Professional Skills For 21st Century

A key to success

Vitthal Gore

BlueRose ONE

Stories Matter

NewDelh • London

BLUEROSE PUBLISHERS
India | U.K.

For permissions requests or inquiries regarding this publication, please contact:

BLUEROSE PUBLISHERS
www.BlueRoseONE.com
info@bluerosepublishers.com
+91 8882 898 898
+4407342408967

ISBN: 978-93-5819-204-9

First Edition: August 2023

Dedicated to

the words of wisdom

of my teachers and mentors

who have blessed me

with knowledge and skills...

Contents

Foreword

Man has been making perennial efforts to chisel his creativity for a meaningful and productive activity, which ultimately leading him to self-satisfaction and joy. After all, skill happens to be one of prerequisites of the modern life. There is no human sphere that doesn't demand a set of skills. In other words, at every step of our life, and in every situation, we need to apply the requisite skills to accomplish any work being undertaken by each one of us. It is an era of specialization, every job demands a special set of skills, and that is how we need to prepare our workforce, and the youngsters in the annals of higher education. We need to use our talents and knowledge in a most judicious way, befitting to the occasion for a higher output and performance. The skills we evolve or generate or acquire could be used in any time. We might create skills in any field, the skills could be the art of creating with ease on any task with expertise and a functional utility, including in writing, speaking and even in listening, or it may be an execution of it in any sphere of human life.

Of course, skills are not necessarily limited only to humans, even animals have been able to train themselves in the art of acquiring certain skills, and some skills have been acquired by them by a diligent training given by humans. The classic example is, how an American researcher Jane Goodall contributed for chimpanzees' protection in their habitats and studied their behavioural pattern and skills and proved that they too can use simple instruments / tools. I am tempted to quote about this great lady for her path breaking research on skills of chimps. So, skills have become so much important that even in our country there is a separate Department and Ministry created by Government of India. There is also the National Skill Development Corporation; moreover, Skill India has become a buzzword. The list of skills may be endless, we can name a few skills - like communication, problem solving, conflict resolution, negotiation, presentation, empathy, team building, analytical, leadership, listening, persuasion, speaking, reading, writing, and the list continues like this.

I am really delighted to pen down a few impressions that I have been able to gather from this book authored by Dr. Vitthal Gore, who is an accomplished writer and an authority on such subjects, as he has been involved for nearly two decades in delivering lectures and deliberating on such topics on several academic forums. This kind of self-exposure has readied him to write a text that is significant for modern world. This book has no boarders, anybody can use it, whether it is a student or teacher or even corporate personnel. All can use it very effectively and grow in their personal life. That is my personal impression as well as my open confession.

As the title itself indicates this book caters to the needs of the citizens / netizens of the 21st century. As the author also claims very rightly, the skills refer to a set of abilities and competencies that are considered essential for individuals to thrive and succeed in the 21stcentury. "These skills are often associated with the demands of the digital age, globalization, and rapidly changing work environments." He also has highlighted on the topics like Critical Thinking and Problem Solving, wherein he stresses on the ability of an individual to "analyse information, evaluate different perspectives, and make reasoned decisions." He also touches on the importance of Collaboration and Communication, stressing on the importance of active listening, clear articulation of ideas, empathy, teamwork, and the ability to collaborate across cultures and time zones. He has eminently focused on the ability of an individual to think creatively, generate new ideas, and apply them to solve problems or create something valuable. In the chapter titled 'Information Literacy' wherein the author foregrounds on digital literacy, media literacy, and the ability to navigate and critically assess the vast amount of information available on the digital platform.

Most importantly he has dealt on a special topic called emotional intelligence, which indeed has a contemporary relevance. The ability to recognize and manage one's own emotions and understand and empathize with others is the need of the hour, I hope everyone agrees it. As per the author, it includes skills like self-awareness, self-regulation, empathy, and effective interpersonal relationships. Similarly, he speaks on the most vital topic in the present day like - Leadership and Responsibility. In this context he lays stress on the capacity to lead and take responsibility and skills in decision-making, ethical behaviour, project management, etc. He devotes a special chapter on Communication Skills on the subjects like listening, speaking, reading and writing as they are the backbone to successes in the present-day globalised world. He also deals with the Non-verbal Communication, Digital Literacy, Professional Skills, the Career Skills such as Résumé Writing, Interview Skills, Group Discussion Skills, Team Skills, Cognitive and Non-cognitive Skills, and Presentation Skills.

In the absence of a good leader and proper managerial support, no one could be successful in life. This chapter talks about Leadership Skills, Managerial Skills and Entrepreneurial Skills. It is very important to notice that he has also composed his inputs on Universal Human Values like Love and Compassion, Truth, Non-violence, Righteousness, Peace, Service etc. which are terribly missing in many spheres of life. These skills are considered essential in preparing individuals to navigate the complexities of the 21st century, whether in education, the workforce, or personal life, asserts the author.

I express my joy over this contribution of authoring a book on vital issues of modern life, by my fellow colleague to the general public. I know words are too little to comprehend Dr. Gore's contribution through this book, but he has achieved this feat with great amount of hard work. Hence, I express my profound sense of gratitude for his accomplishment and wish him all the best for the future endeavours.

Kudos to Dr. Vitthal Gore.

Dr. S. G. Dollegoudar Patil
(Author and Poet)
Dean, Faculty of Languages,
Sharnbasva University, Kalaburagi,
Karnataka, India.
23 June 2023.

Preface

Professional Skills For 21ˢᵗ Century refers to a set of abilities and competencies that are considered crucial for individuals to thrive and succeed in this century. These skills are often associated with the demands of the digital age, globalization, and rapidly changing work environments.

Professional Skills

Professional Skills determine one's path of success in career making. Hence the career skills such as resume skills, interview skills, group discussion skills, exploring career opportunities, cognitive and non-cognitive skills, social and cultural etiquettes, internal communication, etc. have been discussed here.

Critical Thinking and Problem Solving

This chapter deals with the ability of an individual to analyse information, evaluate different perspectives, and make reasoned decisions. It involves identifying problems, developing creative solutions, and adapting to new challenges.

Collaboration and Communication

The second chapter deals with the capacity of an individual to work effectively with others, both in-person and virtually. This skill includes active listening, clear articulation of ideas, empathy, teamwork, and the ability to collaborate across cultures and time zones.

Creativity and Innovation

The chapter focuses on the ability of an individual to think creatively, generate new ideas, and apply them to solve problems or create something valuable. It involves originality, flexibility, and the willingness to take risks.

Information Literacy

The chapter titled 'Information Literacy' makes an attempt to identify the capability of an individual to find, evaluate, and effectively use information from diverse sources. It includes digital literacy, media literacy, and the ability to navigate and critically assess the vast amount of information available in the digital age.

Digital Literacy

The Proficiency in using digital tools and technologies to communicate, collaborate, and access information is discussed in this chapter. This includes skills in digital communication, online safety, data analysis, coding, and familiarity with various software and online platforms.

Social Media

This chapter deals with digital literacy, ethics, cyber security, social media and so on. The knowledge of these fields is inevitable in the technologically advanced world. This chapter will provide adequate information about this realm.

Global Awareness

This chapter illustrates understanding and appreciating cultural diversity, global issues, and interconnectedness. It involves having knowledge about different cultures, languages, and socio-economic conditions, as well as the ability to work effectively in multicultural environments.

Adaptability and Flexibility

The capacity to embrace change, be open to new ideas, and adapt to evolving circumstances is the major focus of this chapter. This skill includes resilience, agility, and the ability to learn and unlearn as needed.

Initiative and Entrepreneurship

The ability to take initiative, be proactive, and pursue opportunities are the points which are discussed in this chapter. It involves a mindset of innovation, risk-taking, and the willingness to create and seize new possibilities.

Emotional Intelligence

This chapter tries to justify the need of emotional intelligence in the modern world; the ability to recognize and manage one's own emotions and understand and empathize with others. It includes skills such as self-awareness, self-regulation, empathy, and effective interpersonal relationships.

Leadership and Responsibility

The capacity to lead and take responsibility for oneself and others are discussed in this chapter. This involves skills in decision-making, ethical behaviour, project management, and the ability to inspire and motivate others.

Communication Skills (LSRW Skills)

LSRW skills are the backbone to success in this global world. This chapter deals with Listening, Speaking, Reading, and Writing independently and also focuses on Nonverbal Communication.

Presentation Skills

Presentation Skills play an important role in the success of an individual. This chapter provides all necessary skills required for an individual in his or her professional life.

Management Skills

In the absence of a good leader and proper managerial support, no one will be successful in life. This chapter focuses on the leadership skills, managerial skills, entrepreneurial skills, innovative leadership and design thinking, ethics and integrity, managing personal finance, etc.

Universal Human Values

The last chapter makes an attempt to deal with a few identified universal human values like - love and compassion, truth, non-violence, righteousness, peace, service, renunciation, constitutional values, justice and human rights.

These skills are considered essential in preparing individuals to navigate the complexities of the 21st century, whether in education, the workforce, or personal life. They emphasize a holistic approach to learning that goes beyond traditional academic knowledge and focuses on equipping individuals with transferable skills that can be applied across various domains.

It gives me immense pleasure to present this book to readers. Hope, it will serve the purpose and provide inputs for holistic development of professional skills among the budding professionals.

Dr. Vitthal Gore
Assistant Professor and Head,
Department of English,
Shri Havagiswami College, Udgir,
Maharashtra, India.
15 August 2023.

Acknowledgments

By the blessings of Lord Venkateshwara and the goodwill of many people around, I could undertake many responsibilities in personal and professional life. One of them is the completion of this book that owes me an extreme degree of indebtedness and appreciation to a host of 'souls-in-deed' for whom my love and respect will ever increase.

I express my sincere gratitude to Mr. Nivrutti Kale Sir Mr. D.L. Deshmukh Sir, Mr. Pandit Sir, Mr. D.G. Kulkarni Sir, Mrs. Kalpana Saraf Madam, Prof. Harihar Kulkarni Sir, Prof. Vivek Giridhari Sir, Prof. Jayashri Mohanraj Madam, Prof. B. Yadava Raju Sir and all my teachers for their valuable guidance and prompt attention. I express my deep sincere gratitude for their words of wisdom which they shared with me.

I would like to proclaim that Mr. Mahesh Pendke, my mentor, who always encourages me for upward growth and helps me at every step for academic development; I am indebted to him for his support and counselling.

I am also thankful to Dr. S. G. Dollegoudar Patil, (Author and Poet) Dean, Faculty of Languages, Sharnbasva University, Kalaburagi, Karnataka for his perfect blend of concerns and guidance which has encouraged me to standardise the content of this book. I also express my sincere gratitude to him for writing Foreword to this book.

I am also indebted to Adv. Gunvantrao Patil Haibatpurkar, President, Bharat Liberal Education Society, Udgir and Mr. Umesh Patil Deonikar, Secretary, Bharat Liberal Education Society, Udgir and all the honourable office bearers and members of Bharat Liberal Education Society, Udgir for their constant encouragement and directorial support.

I would like to express my gratitude to Blue Rose Publishers for providing me a platform by publishing this book and giving me an acknowledgement worldwide.

No thanks can make me free from indebtedness to my parents Late. Mrs. Manorama Gore and Late. Mr. Gangadharrao Gore who are the constant source of motivation.

I am always bound in love and gratitude to my spouse Mrs. Rajashri, and my beloved children Ms. Vedashri and Master Vedant whose silent support made it possible for me to pursue and complete the book. The technical support in cover designing by Master Vedant and typesetting by Ms. Vedashri has made this book technically sound. I also appreciate Ms. Vedashri for her meticulous look at the draft of the book and her intensive reading at the final stage that has made this book errorless.

I also express my gratitude to all my friends, colleagues and well-wishers for their love and support time and again.

Once again, I express my thankfulness to Lord Venkateshwara for cherishing my vision to explore my capability to strive hard for achieving all pinnacles in life.

Dr. Vitthal Gore

15 August 2023

1. Professional Skills

Continuous personal and professional development is your key to the future.

-   Brian Tracy

Professional skills are the qualities and abilities of an individual to perform an assigned task or work or job effectively by collaborating and interacting with others. Hence, professional Skills are also called as workplace skills. While working for any organization, an employee needs certain skill sets to execute his/her job/work/duty/task as per the profile but in order to perform the same, the employee is expected to be well trained and well informed for certain professional skills so that the assigned work will be executed systematically and successfully. Apart from the professional skills there are technical skills also. Technical skills are specific to a particular field or job. The technical skills can be developed by providing training for a period of time but the professional skills need a personal attention by the employee for a longer period of time. The technical and professional skills are applicable and transferable across various industries and multinational corporations.

The following sections deal with a few identified professional skills:

1. **Resume Skills**

Before entering any organization as an employee, it is your resume that forms your image in front of the recruiters. Resume skills are the core competencies and they are specific abilities and the domains of knowledge which can be highlighted by an individual along with the academic qualifications and certifications. In order to sustain a job, relevant skills help employers to assess the capabilities of the aspirant and determine whether the candidate is suitable for the job or not.

a. Identify relevant skills

An aspirant should take a review of the job description and make some research about the organization to identify the important skills the employer is looking for. An aspirant should always think of his/her own skill sets seriously and consider both technical skills and professional as required for the employer.

b. Tailor your skills

Each job demands certain skills, so always update and customize your resume by emphasizing the skill sets required for the specific job. Priority should be given the specifically identified skills in order to make a strong impression on the potential employer.

c. Categorise your skills

An aspirant should to be aware of the demands of the industry and the potential employer. Every job is unique and needs some skills, so categorise your skills under certain heads like technical skills, communication skills, problem-solving skills, software proficiency, etc.

d. Use action words

An aspirant should bring his / her skill sets to the notice of the potential employer. So, start each skill statement with strong action verbs and make your skills standout. Don't simply state 'Microsoft Word or Excel', it is better to write 'Proficient in Microsoft Word or Excel for data analysis and reporting'. Likewise, do it with other important skills and make an effort to impress the potential employer through your resume.

e. Provide evidence

While writing about your skills and achievements provide specific examples in nutshell. It will enable the employer to check your performance based on the evidence that you have produced. Provide some details of the assignment that you have completed in the current or previous organizations and extended profit to the organization and satisfaction to the client.

f. Quantify your skills

Wherever possible, do quantify your skills. Actually, by quantifying your skills, you create an impression on the employer. Don't simply mention that you have 'customer service skills', if you are experienced mention that you have handled approximately 50 inquiries in a day with 95% of the satisfaction rating'. It will create an impression on the potential employer.

g. Balance technical skills and soft skills

Each job demands a few specific skills, so try to make a balance between your technical skills and soft skills that you mention in your resume. Depending on the job, make a proper mix of technical and soft skills to showcase your competence and other abilities. Highlighting soft skills like communication, teamwork, problem-solving and adaptability would have some value.

h. Keep it concise

While writing your resume, do not dump each and every detail about you in the draft. Be concise and focus only on the most important and relevant skills. Always aim for the targeted resume and prioritize the skills that can differentiate you from others and increase your possibility of getting selected.

i. Update and revise

Time and again, review and revise your resume, more particularly your skill set section. Your skill sets should align properly with your objective statement. In the course of experience, you keep on upgrading your skills, so keep updating your resume also. It creates a positive impression on the potential employer and shows that you are constantly improving yourself as a professional.

While drafting resume, the aspirant should always remember that he should be truthful to the content that he writes in the resume. Always support and provide some evidence for your claims, don't be over admirable for the self. The resume should reflect your professional personality through a document. So, increase possibility of getting noticed by the potential employer by your effective resume writing skill.

2. Group Discussion Skills

Group discussions are very crucial in academic and professional settings. Group discussions provide an opportunity to every participant to exchange ideas, thoughts, and collaborate to reach to a conclusion. In the modern times, many corporate companies use group discussion as a tool for short listing aspirants for various jobs. The aspirant's communication skills, team building skills, collaborative approach and adaptability are being monitored. So, group discussions play important role in the career making of many individuals.

The following sections provide a few tips to improve group discussion skills:

a. Preparation

The topic of group discussion demands preparation, so familiarise yourself with the topic or the agenda beforehand. Collect the relevant information, facts, and opinions to support your arguments. In addition, do some research about the topic that will also enable you for making your strong arguments and contribution.

b. Active listening

While participating in a group discussion, one should pay full attention to the discussion and be an active listener. It will enable you to make your arguments and justify. Avoid internal and external interruptions and genuinely engage with what others say. Take your running notes which may help you for further discussion.

c. Courteous communication

During the discussion, respectful and courteous language plays a crucial role to form your image as a good participant. One should always give extreme respect to the counterparts and use effective suitable, courteous language for others. Never use derogative language and don't make any personal attack on any participant. Begin your statements with the pronoun 'I' for expressing your own thoughts and experiences. It is suggested not to just make statements having assumptions and generalizations.

d. Constructive participation

Active participation can bring your attempt to the notice of the monitor. Constructively participate in the proceedings of the group discussion and make your attempt meaningful. Share your ideas, thoughts, perspectives, experiences, and insights and support them with examples and evidences. Similarly, encourage others to participate and play a leading role. Ask thoughtful questions and queries and try to seek clarifications when necessary.

e. Collaboration and building on ideas

If you want to perform a leading role in the group discussion, adopt collaborative approach and be inclusive during the proceedings. Never dismiss or disregard ideas and thoughts shared by others but find other ways out to induct your stand in amicable manner. Build on your thoughts based on the ideas shared by others and contribute to collective thinking of the group.

f. Time management

A session of group discussion is allotted with a specific time period. Everyone should take an opportunity to constructively contribute and complete the discussion with a conclusion within the allocated time. So, be time bound, allow everybody to contribute, never dominate and take the entire time allocated. One should always stay focused and avoid deviation of topic. If it happens during the discussion, try to bring everybody back to the topic.

g. Non-verbal communication

Non-Verbal communication supports verbal communication. It is said that action speaks louder than words. So, never underestimate non-verbal cues, kinesics, body language, movements, etc. They immensely contribute to the success of the group discussion. The level of confidence can be checked and evaluated by the monitor based on non-verbal cues and so on. So, maintain proper eye contact, keep up your moral high, use proper body language, and be an active participant.

h. Flexibility and adaptability

In the course of group discussion, don't stick up to your view point. Be flexible and adjust with others. Avoid rigid thinking and be open to accept common ideas and conclusions drawn collectively.

i. Synthesizing and summarizing

Synthesizing allows a participant to combine different ideas and perspectives of participants to help the group search for conclusions and identify probable areas of agreement.

Summarizing allows a participant to summarize the main points and ensure that all the participants are on the same line of thinking about the topic. This also allows all the participants to come to some conclusion.

j. Reflect and learn

After the discussion is over, speculate over your performance, find out the areas for improvement, and learn from the experience. Reflecting and learning should be a continuous process and it should go on till one feels that s/he has reached to a certain level and performs better.

Altogether, group discussion is tool which is extensively used by the incorporation especially during the recruitment process. So, in order to succeed in group discussion, one should to be well prepared and have a common objective to achieve. One should participate actively, listen carefully, reflect sensibly and conclude systematically.

3. Interview Skills

An interview is a scheduled formal meeting between the aspirant candidate for a job and a panel of experts formed for the purpose of recruitment on the behalf of an organization. In the modern times, interview skills are essential for an aspiring candidate for effectively presenting his or her qualifications, domain knowledge, soft and hard skills to prove suitability for a particular job.

In order to improve the interview skills, a few tips have been provided in the following sections. These skills will help a candidate to crack the hard nut:

a. Research the organization

Once you decide to apply for a particular job lying vacant in an organization, start doing research about the organization thoroughly. Before appearing the interview, the knowledge about the organization, it's standing in the market, reputation, balance sheet, profit margin, its competitors, mission, values, recent news, and the domain of works and projects will help a lot to formulate your answers in the interview. This information will help you to tailor made your responses and demonstrate your interest in the organization. Automatically, this approach and preparation may enhance your chances of getting an opportunity.

b. Understand the job requirements

Pre-interview preparation helps the candidate to crack the hard nut easily. So, make an effort to understand the job description and requirements in terms of qualification, domain knowledge, and skill sets. During the interview, always reflect on how your experience and skills will be helpful for the growth of the organization. If possible, illustrate with an example about your abilities and result oriented performance.

c. Practice common interview questions

There are a few common interview questions like 'introduce yourself', 'why are you interested in this job?', 'what are your strengths and weaknesses?', 'how will you contribute to the growth of this organization?', etc. With a meticulous understanding about the mission and values of the organization, a candidate should prepare and practice these questions so that impressive and effective responses can be given in the interview. Special focus is needed for question on 'SWOT' – Strengths, Weaknesses, Opportunities, and Threats. Your answer to this question should be so logical that all the four elements should support one another. Similarly use STAR (Situation, Task, Action, and Result) method to structure your responses.

d. Showcase your achievements

Your resume reflects your qualifications, experience, skills and achievements. But during the interview, a candidate should talk about the same effectively and illustrate along with a few selected examples. It would be better to quantify your answers related to your achievements and quality measures which may bring a difference in the notice of the expert's panel.

e. Practice listening skills

During the interview, be attentive and pay active attention to the questions asked by the interviewers. Before answering, compose yourself, your thoughts, take a long breath and answer in cool and calm way. Never show your anxiety and uneasiness. Be comfortable, directly answer the question and provide relevant information. Never move around the bush, always talk something of value and sense.

f. Demonstrate professionalism

Professional approach during the interview is desperately needed. A candidate is expected to be well-groomed, professionally dressed-up, and maintain positive body language, tone, and eye contact. Be punctual, arrive on time and be focused during the interview.

g. Ask thoughtful questions and queries

Asking thoughtful and sensible questions is a skill. In the course of work experience, people learn this skill. It is advised to demonstrate your interest and role in the company if you are provided with the opportunity. Prepare a set of questions to be asked to the interviewers. It is better to ask about the company culture, opportunities of growth, project related questions, etc.

h. Show your enthusiasm

Be very specific about your career goals; show your genuine interest in the opportunity and the company. Keep up your morale high and talk about your aspirations if you are given the opportunity.

i. Follow up with a Thank You note

After the interview, never forget to send an email expressing your personalized note of thanks. Express your gratitude for the opportunity of facing the interview and share your experience there. It is suggested to reiterate your interest in the company and ensure them about your performance and result oriented approach.

j. Reflect and learn

After the interview, reflect on the interview session as a whole and speculate about your performance in the view of the interviewers. Being a candidate, you may feel good about your performance but other's perspectives are equally important to balance it. Similarly, use this feedback and self-assessment for your personal improvement in the upcoming interviews.

Practice makes man perfect. So, remember, it is the practice that can prepare you thoroughly. Take the help of a mentor or friend and practice your answers, monitor your body language, etc. It will help you to perform better.

In most of the organizations, the process of recruitment is conducted through short listing resumes, group discussions, then followed by a personal interview. Those who qualify these three stages may have some future prospects with the organization. So, every aspirant is expected to be well read, prepared and cautious of the professional requirements and provide the same as and when needed and demanded for the growth of the organization. Never forget that the growth of the organization is equal to the growth of the employee and vice versa.

4. Career Skills

Each job is different in nature and work profile. So, developing career making skills have become crucial for everyone aspirant for a new opportunity. Career skills are also known as job specific skills or hard skills like technical abilities and domain knowledge required to perform a particular job. These skills are typically acquired through education, training, on job experience, or exposure to certain work profile. There are numerous career skills depending on the field or work profile but a few can be enlisted for a general awareness. A few examples of career skills across different industries are as follows:

- ✓ Information Technology (IT)
- ✓ Programming languages (Java, Python, C++)
- ✓ Web development (HTML, CSS, JavaScript)
- ✓ Database management (SQL, MySQL)
- ✓ Network administration and security
- ✓ Systems analysis and design
- ✓ IT project management
- ✓ Software proficiency

- Healthcare
- Medical terminology and transcription
- Patient assessment and diagnosis
- Medical procedures (phlebotomy, CPR)
- Electronic health records (EHR) systems
- Medical coding and billing
- Health informatics
- Finance and Accounting
- Financial analysis and reporting
- Budgeting and forecasting
- Auditing and compliance
- Taxation and tax planning
- Financial modelling and valuation
- Risk management
- Marketing and Advertising
- Market research and analysis
- Digital marketing (SEO, SEM, social media)
- Brand management
- Advertising campaign planning and execution
- Content creation and copywriting
- Data analytics and metrics tracking
- Core Engineering (Electrical, or civil engineering)
- CAD/CAM software proficiency
- Project management

- ✓ Problem-solving and designing skills
- ✓ Technical drawing and blueprint interpretation
- ✓ Quality control and testing
- ✓ Sales and Customer Service
- ✓ Sales techniques and strategies
- ✓ Relationship building and customer management
- ✓ Negotiation and persuasion skills
- ✓ Product knowledge and demonstrations
- ✓ Complaint handling and conflict resolution
- ✓ Education
- ✓ Curriculum development
- ✓ Classroom management
- ✓ Instructional design and lesson planning
- ✓ Assessment and evaluation
- ✓ Special education techniques
- ✓ Technology integration in teaching
- ✓ Human Resources (HR)
- ✓ Recruitment and selection
- ✓ Employee on boarding and orientation
- ✓ HR policies and compliance
- ✓ Performance management
- ✓ Employee relations and conflict resolution
- ✓ Training and development and so on.

The list can be exhaustive but in order to understand different career skills across different industries, this list has been provided. These examples highlight specific career skills, but it's important to note that many job roles require a combination of both career skills and the professional skills mentioned earlier, such as communication, problem-solving, and teamwork. Developing a strong foundation of career skills relevant to your chosen profession is crucial for success and advancement within your career. Continual learning, staying updated with industry trends, and acquiring new skills are also important for adapting to the evolving demands of the job market.

a. Exploring career opportunities

Exploring career opportunities is a crucial step in finding a job, fulfilling the requirements, and beginning with a suitable career. There are some steps and strategies to help in this process. If an aspiring candidate looks into these strategies carefully, it may help him or her in career making.

The strategies like, self-reflection, research, networking, internships and volunteering, skill development, seeking guidance, experiment and take risks, set goals and create a plan, evaluate and adapt, team building skills, communication, collaboration, relationship building, flexibility and adaptability, problem-solving, decision-making, conflict resolution, time management, leadership, accountability, etc. make a big difference.

b. Cognitive skills

There are two broad categories of skills which contribute to overall development of an individual. To succeed in professional life, an individual should develop several skill sets. The cognitive skills refer to the personal abilities of an individual and process related to acquiring, processing, and applying knowledge. These skills involve the use of memory, intellect, critical thinking, and decision-making.

The examples of cognitive skills are logical reasoning, attention and concentration, memory, information processing, analytical thinking, problem-solving, and creativity.

c. **Non-cognitive skills**

Non-cognitive skills encompass a range of personal qualities, attitudes, behaviours, etc. which may influence others during the interactions. Socio-emotional skills or soft skills are also called as non-cognitive skills. These skills manage emotions, behaviours, social interactions, etc.

The examples of non-cognitive skills are communication, teamwork and collaboration, emotional intelligence, self-awareness, adaptability and resilience, leadership, time management and conflict resolution.

Cognitive and non-cognitive skills are essential for holistic development of an individual. Both the skills considerably contribute to the success of an individual. They are complementary to each other and equally contribute in the making of a personality. These skills can lead a personal growth, improved academic and professional performance and enhanced well-being.

This chapter mainly focused on the resume skills, group discussion, interview skill and the cognitive and non-cognitive skills in general. This leading chapter does not talk about all the skills called 'Professional Skills'. The main objective of this book is to highlight the professional skills which are required in the 21ˢᵗ century. Henceforth the chapters included in this book deal with diverse professional skills required in the job market in the 21ˢᵗ century.

2. Critical Thinking and Problem Solving

We cannot solve our problems with the same thinking we used when we created them.

- Albert Einstein

Critical thinking and problem solving are the fundamental skills of all times. 21stCentury demands every professional to be very particular about thinking out of the box and critically looks at the problems and solve them in effective ways. Analysing information, evaluating evidences, making logical decisions, are generally involved in the entire process of critical thinking and problem solving. These skills are the prerequisites for the 21st century jobs because the challenges and complexities are different so are the problem-solving techniques.

1. Analysis

The process of critical thinking involves the analysis of complex information into its constituent parts. The process also examines all the internal and external aspects in detail. Such an attempt requires an ability to identify the key elements, interconnected relationships and patterns within a problem. The holistic understanding of a problem enables an individual to solve it.

In order to come to well-reasoned judgements or decisions, the analysis of the problem and a critical approach to address it plays an important role. While analysing information and ideas, systematic and objective approach becomes a decisive factor. It is a crucial component and refers to the process of examining and breaking down complex ideas, arguments, situations and other integral aspects into their constituent parts in order to understand the structure, pattern, relationship and its implications. The stages of analysing a problem and address the same with a critical approach typically involves the following steps:

a. Understanding the problem

Right in the beginning, clearly identifying the problem, issue or question is necessary for successful attempt of solving the problem. In depth understanding of the issue or question generally enables an individual to define its core, key terms, pattern, and so on. So always be patient to understand the problem.

b. Gathering relevant information

After having proper comprehension of the problem, one should try to collect most relevant information pertinent to the issue. A very reasoned look at the gathered information, data, evidences, etc. will be decisive in the entire process.

c. Identifying assumptions

After a meticulous analysis of the problem, try to recognize any underlying assumptions or presuppositions that may be present in the gathered information. Similarly try to determine whether the assumptions are reasonable, valid, and unbiased.

d. Evaluating evidences

Proper examination of the sources, methodology, analysis and fact finding enables an individual to assess the credibility, reliability and the authenticity of the entire process. So be very particular during this process and double check and evaluate the evidences. Any error at this stage may cost heavier later.

e. Identifying logical reasoning

First of all, make an attempt to analyse the logical structure of the claims being presented and the arguments made. The supporting statements and the conclusions drawn provide a better stance to an individual to address the problem logically. In addition, proper evaluation of the logical validity and coherence of the reasoning will also help to solve it tactfully.

f. Identifying strengths and weaknesses

The information gathered should be analysed logically by considering its strengths and weaknesses. Always consider counterarguments and alternative explanations whenever required. Similarly assess any potential fallacies, biases, gaps, etc. in order to address them meticulously.

g. Drawing conclusions

After the meticulous analysis of the information, data, arguments, counterarguments make an effort to draw well-supported logical conclusions and judgements. Double ensure that the conclusions and judgements are properly supported with acceptable reasoning and evidences.

h. Reflecting on implications

Always have a broader perspective to the implications and consequences of the conclusions drawn. Remember that the process of analysis and conclusions do influence decision making and plays a decisive role in its consequences.

In nutshell, one should understand that critical thinking and problem solving require an open-minded objective approach. Any kind of personal biases, viewpoints, prejudices, etc. severally affect the entire process and it largely disturbs the decision process as well. So, in order to develop strong critical thinking and problem-solving abilities, one should practice it till you refine your analytical skills and put the same in to action.

2. Evaluation

Basically, critical thinking distinguishes between the fact and opinion. It involves the process of assessing information, validity, reliability, credibility of information and sources. Similarly, evaluation forms a crucial aspect of the entire process. Assessing quality, value, arguments, counterarguments, actions, assumptions, conclusions, etc. are critically evaluated in this process. It is a process of forming judgements, making judgements, purely based on analysis, evidence, reasoning, and so on. Evaluation is a decisive factor and it helps to determine the strengths, weaknesses, credibility, and authenticity. In the entire process of evaluation, the following elements are involved:

a. Relevance

Ensure that the information and data collected is relevant to problem or question at hand. Avoid to store or keep irrelevant data, it may affect the whole process later.

b. Credibility

The information gathered through reliable sources will automatically create credibility about it. While gathering information and collecting data, a professional should check accuracy, trustworthiness, and reliability of the sources which will enhance the credibility.

c. Validity

An attempt should be made to examine the validity of the arguments. Evaluate the reliability of the reasoning, strength of the evidence and overall coherence. Also put in your efforts to identify the fallacies or errors if any.

d. Consistency

Check the established facts, information gathered and the arguments made in the respect of the problem. Similarly assess the consistency and determine whether there are any contradictions, inconsistencies, or conflicts with other reliable sources.

e. Bias and perspective

A proper evaluation of the information is necessary in order to check whether it is balanced, consistent, objective or slanted. Try to recognize any biases, assumptions, or perspectives which may influence the processed information. Always consider the potential motivational factors behind the information presented.

f. Context

While dealing with any problem, it is necessary to consider the historical, cultural, social, situational factors which influence the information or the argument. Similarly try to determine whether any context affects the validity or the relevance of the information.

g. Consequences

The entire process of critical thinking and problem solving will have its own consequences. If everything goes in the right directed with a logical outcome, consequences will be positive otherwise it will have reverse effect. So always assess the potential consequences, rely upon the information gathered, have a broad perspective with an objective approach. Check whether your conclusions are based on the evaluation.

h. Judgement

Reflective thinking allows an individual to form well-reasoned judgements based on the process of logical evaluation. Always keep it in mind that alternative perspectives, counter arguments, limitations of the evaluations may help you a lot in order to come to certain judgement with a logical concern.

In nut shell, it can be said that evaluation process in critical thinking and problem solving requires a thoughtful and systematic approach. Evaluating objectives, assumptions, problem identification, logical approach, techniques, problem solving, etc. are the decisive factors. Developing strong evaluation skills are also essential for distinguishing between reliable and unreliable information and successfully solving the problem.

3. Problem-Solving Strategies

There are a few problem-solving strategies which can be adopted while addressing a problem. Critical thinking helps in developing these skills. The strategies such as breaking down complex problem into smaller, manageable parts, speculating and brainstorming ideas, pondering alternative perspectives, systematic approach to potential solutions, etc. are required for solving-problems. These strategies are different approaches and techniques used to identify, analyse, and solve a problem effectively. In addition, a structured framework is also provided in order to tackle complex and challenging problems and issues. There are a few problem-solving strategies like defining a problem, gathering information, analysing a problem, generating a possible solution, evaluating options, developing an action plan, opting the best solution, implementing the opted solution, evaluating the results, refining the whole process, and so on.

Here it is important to note that these strategies can be adapted and tailored to different situations. In the entire process, critical thinking, creativity, and flexibility are very much essential for effective problem solving.

As problems, obstacles, hindrances are inevitable, practice, exposure and diverse perspectives are important factors for developing critical thinking and problem solving. If one has strong willingness to acquire these skills, mastering the skills and implementing the same in different situations will not be much challenging. In the 21st century, these skills are highly valued in academics and professional set up.

3. Collaboration and Communication

The original idea of the web was that it should be a collaborative space where you can communicate through sharing information.

-   Tim Berners-Lee

Collaboration and communication are crucial professional skills. In the present sophisticated modern world, working in a team and maintaining effective communication and collaboration are essential skills in various settings. Together Everyone Achieves More (TEAM) is the principle of collaborative work and mastery over effective communication which play a pivotal role in an organization in order to achieve its goals.

1. Collaboration

Collaboration is essentially a process which demands a group of professionals coming together to achieve a common goal. It encourages everyone in a team to contribute his or her knowledge, skills, information, and put in very sincere efforts in order to attain a shared outcome. This process involves an active cooperation and dedicated participation of every individual of a team who should be inclined to contribute his or her unique expertise, perspectives, and resources to achieve the short term and ultimate goals. Since the advent of multinational companies, this professional skill has received countless importance.

The following section deals with a few characteristics of this principle:

a. Cooperation and teamwork

Working in isolation is obsolete now. All the organizations want their employees to have a collaborative approach and extend their cooperation to the members of their team and be spirited to achieve the common goal with effective communication. Every individual is expected to be involved actively and team up with the rest to prove their team as an entity and support the collaborative effort.

b. Communication and open dialogue

The first principle of collaboration is transparent and open communication with the team members. It requires sharing information, ideas, opinions, suggestions, feedback and so on to foster better understanding among the members and proper alignment at intellectual level.

c. Trust and respect

The concept of collaboration fundamentally demands vote of trust for one another among all the members of a team. Vote of trust creates respect and honour for the rest and also creates conducive environment and healthy work atmosphere in the team. Proper communication, better mutual understanding, building mutual trust and rapport are the essential factors for success.

d. Interdependence

Each member of a team should never forget that s/he is a part and parcel of an entity called a team. Fundamentally a team requires support and cooperation of all the inmates. Here each member should remember that s/he cannot perform better in isolation unless supported by others. It means that s/he is interdependent. This principle of interdependence teaches an individual to rely on others and trust for the sake of common goal. Success of the team is possible only when all the team members work as a team to achieve collective goals.

e. Conflict resolution

Difference of opinion, disagreement and conflicts are always inevitable. Collaboration acknowledges such conflicts which may arise while working in a team. Such conflicts should be structurally addressed and nullified by coming to a common understanding and by seeking a win-win situation. Conflict should never reach to breakup in professional relationship but it should maintain positive professional relationship.

f. Sharing resources

Different resources are required for a team while working in collaboration. Pooling and sharing resources whether they are physical resources, expertise opinions, information, human resource networks, etc. do contribute in a team.

g. Common goal

In team collaboration, an individual contributes independently but for a shared goal which is to be achieved collectively by all. The real collaboration happens when different individuals come together to pursue a common objective and put in their committed efforts to achieve the goals.

h. Flexibility and adaptability

While working in a team with a collaborative approach, everyone should have a willingness to be flexible and adaptable in response to the changing circumstances. All the members need to adjust to changing roles, information, situations, and so on. One fixed formula can never work for expected gaols.

These are the key characteristics of collaboration. It is commonly observed in all types of settings such as professional, academic, community initiatives, research projects, and problem-solving contexts. Collaboration takes various forms like formal, informal, small-scale, large-scale collaborations and so on. Working in collaboration for attaining certain common goals is mostly successful because multiple minds work on one particular goal to achieve. There are several benefits of working in collaboration. Increased creativity, innovativeness, problem-solving capabilities, diverse perspectives, enhanced knowledge and skills, productively, network building, etc.

2. Communication

Communication is a process of exchanging ideas, messages, information, thoughts, emotions, and experiences between individuals or groups or to the masses through various means. Communication involves creating, transmitting, sharing, receiving, interpreting, messages. Effective and successful communication is required in personal and professional life. It is a valuable skill set and every individual should acquire it. It plays an important role in conveying thoughts, expressing feelings, sharing experiences and knowledge, building relationship and so on. This skill set has a few key elements like sender, message, channel, receiver, context, feedback, etc.

a. Sender

The sender is a person who initiates the process of communication by transmitting or encoding a message to the receiver. The role of a sender is to convey or communicate the message or information or ideas effectively to the expected receiver.

b. Message

The message is a kind of information, idea, thought, content, experience, feeling, etc. which a sender intends to convey to the expected recipient. The message can be communicated in different forms like verbal, written, non-verbal, visual, auditory, etc. Verbal messages are spoken words; written messages are written or printed content; non-verbal messages are conveyed through body language, gestures, facial expressions, kinesics; visual messages are conveyed through images, graphs, charts, etc.; auditory messages are conveyed through sounds or tones.

c. Channel

A kind of medium through which a message is transmitted is called channel. There are different mediums to transmit a message. Face-to-face conversations, written documents, telephonic conversations, emails, video conferencing, social media, any other electronic media or print media that facilitates successful transmission of a message.

d. Receiver

Receiver is an individual or an entity that receives the message conveyed or communicated by the sender. The receiver decodes the message and interprets and understands the message accurately.

e. Feedback

In the process of communication, feedback and confirmation by the receiver is very important. The response given by the recipient to the message sender ensures the sender about the delivery and proper comprehension of the same.

f. Context

There are several factors which influence the process of communication. The physical environment, social norms, institutional profiles, professional dealings and relationship, personal approach, etc. play crucial role in the process.

g. Barriers

There are three types of barriers which generally create hindrance in the process of communication - the physical barriers (background noise, technical problems, network issues, etc.), psychological barriers (prejudices, biases, pre-occupied ideas or notions, personal judgements, etc.), and semantic barriers (jargons, language barriers, linguistic issues, etc.). These are detrimental for the success of communication and transmitting any message.

By considering all these key elements of communication, one has to understand that communication is successful only when the message is being understood by the recipient with same contextual meaning as it has been sent by the sender. Effective communication involves the aspects like clarity, conciseness, active perception by the receiver; whether it is by active listening or reading. One should avoid ambiguity while sending a message so that the recipient will receive and understand it without any difficulty. Use appropriate language, keep a positive tone, be clear while texting a message. Similarly on the part a recipient, the message should be properly decoded and comprehension should be correct. Focus on the context of the message, give proper feedback, seek further information if needed, be an active listener or reader.

3. Non-verbal communication

Verbal and written communication is organised by a language. There are hundreds of languages used in the world and communication is established by using a specific language. When it comes to non-verbal communication, we don't need any language but have to understand the body language, posture, movements, gestures, facial expressions, eye contact, and tone of the voice. In face-to-face communications our messages are sent at two levels simultaneously. If the non-verbal cues and the spoken messages are incongruous, the flow of communication is hindered.

The proverb in English - Action speaks louder than words – is quite apt and suggestive to deal with non-verbal communication. Non-verbal cues like body language, facial expressions, gestures, optical glances, kinesics, body, leg and hand movements do convey strongly along with the verbal communication. In order to enhance the quality of communication to next level, we should know how to use non-verbal cues.

a. Categories of non-verbal communication

Porter (2011) divides non-verbal communication into four categories:

✓ **Physical:** This is a personal type of communication. It includes facial expressions, tone of voice, sense of touch, sense of smell, and body movements.

✓ **Aesthetic:** This is a type of communication takes place through creative expressions like playing instrumental music, dancing, painting and sculpturing, etc.

✓ **Signs:** This is a mechanical type of communication which includes the use of signals, flags, the 21-gun salute, horns, sirens, etc.

✓ **Symbolic:** This is a type of communication that makes use of religious, status, or ego-building symbols.

b. Features of non-verbal communication

✓ **Static features:** The static features mainly consist of distance, orientation, postures, and physical contacts.

✓ **Dynamic features:** The dynamic features are facial expressions, eye contact, gestures, glance, kinesics, forward and backward movements, vertical movements, side-to-side movements, personal space.

Basically, non-verbal communication is one of the key aspects of communication and especially useful in a high-context culture. It has multiple functions like regulating and complementing the verbal messages but as a whole it largely contributes to the process of communication.

4. Creativity and Innovation

Deep silence is the mother of Creativity. No creativity can come out of one who is too busy, worried, over-ambitious or lethargic.

-   Sri Sri Ravi Shankar

Creativity and innovation are essential professional skills required in the 21st century. These skills basically involve generating new original ideas, thinking out of the box, applying new solutions to problems, and so on. In this sophisticated modern world, every professional should develop these skills and hone them for personal and professional growth. Those who work in an organization as employees have to be creative and innovative to prove their ability better as compared to others. In the following sections, an attempt is made to understand various intrinsic aspects of creativity and innovation:

1. Creativity

Creativity is considered as a gift of nature to human beings. There are several people who are very creative in their approach and always keep sharing their creativity in various forms. Creativity is a professional skill that refers to the ability of an individual who can generate original and valuable ideas, solutions, and contribute something unique. It combines his/her knowledge, experiences, insights in the form of new ideas or thoughts or processes, etc. This creative approach contributes immensely to the growth of an individual and organization as well.

In order to understand the concept of creativity, we need to know the important characteristics of creativity which are enlisted below:

a. Originality

Originality of ideas, concepts, thoughts, expressions, etc. can be from somebody's unique contribution. Creativity and originality usually involve breaking away from the traditional or conventional thinking. It shows one's different perspective to life and work.

b. Novelty

Novelty is nothing but the quality of being original or new with some unique qualities. Creative ideas and provided solutions involve fresh perspectives and approaches. An approach with novelty is always wanted and accepted.

c. Value

Creativity always adds value to something which is enhanced. Creativity is one step ahead to mere novelty and originality. Creative outcome should add value to something new generated or created. Then, only the contribution will have a meaning with utility value of its own. Sometimes creative outcome may be aesthetically pretty, thought provoking and will have an impact. So, value caries significance.

d. Imagination

Imagination is the visualization or simulation of some novel objects, ideas, sensations, in one's mind which is beyond the reach of five human senses. Creativity is injected by imagination and the ability of an individual to think beyond the constraints of others and explore new ideas without any limitations.

e. Openness and flexibility

In general, creative individuals are open-minded. They are positive about exploring something new and experiment in life. Their openness to learning makes them flexible also.

f. Risk taking

Creative people have ability to take challenges in life. They think that taking risk will give them lead in life. This creative lead makes them different than others. These people challenge the established norms, try to explore unexplored and also accept the possibility of failure in the pursuit of creative and new ideas.

g. Curiosity and inquisitiveness

Individuals with creative mind possess a sense of curiosity. They have thrust for knowledge and always keep themselves involved in some or the other creative activity which is fruitful. They are curious to explore new areas which are unexplored.

Creativity, as said earlier is a nature's gift to an individual, but it can be developed and nurtured in anybody who is open to acquire this skill. It can be acquired by creating conducive atmosphere around, by fostering and encouraging exploration and experimentation, by promoting curiosity, by seeking inspiration from others and other sources, by embracing various means, a growth mindset and values. Creativity incorporates various forms of expressions like artistic creations, designing, inventions, discovery, etc. So, effective communication of creative ideas and thoughts is essential. Mostly it is observed that something creative and innovative is discouraged. Actually, creativity plays a vital role in our professional life today. There is no domain which does not require this skill. The domains like arts, sciences, business, technology, education, etc. need very creative and innovative minds.

2. Innovation

Innovation is a term that refers to a process of the research and development of a commercial or non-commercial product, services, needs, demands, or problem solving in a novel way. It transforms creative ideas into experimental or practical products and adds value to it. A few key aspects of innovation which we should be taken into consideration are as follows:

a. Novelty

Introducing something new or different than others is called novelty. It may involve introducing the entire innovative concept, idea, approach or new elements adding value to the existing one. Novelty is always positively accepted if it meets its basic requirements.

b. Value addition

Value addition mainly focuses on adding genuine value to the innovation done. Any innovation aims to address some or the other need, problem, product, or introducing new concept or idea. The value addition determines the outcome of the innovation which is useful at large for mankind, focused for a group/organization or it has a larger value.

c. Implementation

Innovation should be supported by practical implementation. Implementation involves novice concepts to be implemented effectively in order to extend the benefit to all. Only novice ideas, innovation and value addition cannot make the process successful. So, implementation has a crucial role to play.

d. Improvement

Improvement is an ongoing process and it should go on without any hurdles. Any improvement indicates the liveliness of a process. Innovation is also the same ongoing process and it encourages iterative and continuous improvement. Human mind seeks a constant improvement and betterment of doing things.

e. Creativity and problem-solving

Any kind innovation fundamentally relies on the creative thinking and problem-solving. As mentioned earlier, this skill actually generates new ideas, concepts, and encourages novelty in products, systems, processes, etc. Similarly, problems are inevitable in every organization; so, handling the problems skilfully and solving them with all possible innovative and creative approach is necessary.

f. Multidisciplinary approaches

The fundamental quality of innovation is diverse perspectives and multidisciplinary approaches. This approach to innovation can foster cross-pollination of ideas, concepts, and creativity and promote a holistic approach to solving problems.

g. Risk taking

Bigger the risk likewise the profit – is the principle of modern business. In innovation also, calculated risk taking and embracing uncertainty are the part of the process. In addition, new experiments with new ideas, methods, and technologies are also required for its success.

h. Social impact

The prime aim of innovation is to create a positive influence on business, industries, market, and society as well. Innovation may lead to diverse growth, social progress, healthy competition, and improved quality of human life. It also has its desirable outcomes which are noticeable to the people around. Innovation is a very vast and diverse concept which can occur in the domains like science, business, technology, product designing, social initiatives, problem solving, and so on. It plays a pivotal role in emerging trends, advancement in scientific and technological advancement, and business.

Cultivating the environment of creativity and innovation can foster diverse thinking, experimentation, multidisciplinary collaboration, encouraging the work culture of taking risk, learning from failure, and so on. Such approach to creativity and innovation is valuable across all the domains from business to science, arts, technology, and so on. These skills empower an individual to take positive initiatives in order to adapt the ever-changing challenges of the 21st century jobs and businesses.

5. Information Literacy

Never believe all that you hear.
Always verify the original source of information.

- Lailah Gifty Akita

Information Literacy is a critical 21st century skill that involves the ability to find, evaluate, and effectively use information from various sources. In the era of abundant information, it is essential to develop the skills necessary to navigate and make sense of the vast amount of information available.

Information obtained from various sources can be effectively used for information literacy in order to refer to the ability to identify, locate, evaluate. It encompasses a set of skills, knowledge, and attitudes that enable individuals to navigate the vast amount of information available and make informed decisions.

Information literacy is essential in today's digital age, where information is abundant, easily accessible, and constantly evolving. It empowers individuals to make informed decisions, think critically, solve problems, and participate effectively in social, academic, and professional contexts.

Information literacy skills are particularly crucial in academic settings for conducting research, evaluating scholarly sources, and producing high-quality work. They are also essential in the workplace for staying up-to-date with industry trends, making informed business decisions, and effectively utilizing information resources.

Educational institutions, libraries, and information organizations play a vital role in promoting information literacy by offering instructions, resources, and support to help individuals develop these skills.

The following sections take an insight into information literacy:

1. Information seeking

Information literacy involves effectively identifying and accessing relevant information. It includes the ability to define information needs, formulate search strategies, and utilize appropriate search tools and techniques.

2. Evaluation and critical analysis

Information literacy encompasses the skill of critically evaluating information for credibility, accuracy, bias, and relevance. It involves distinguishing between reliable sources and misinformation or fake news.

3. Source credibility

Information literacy requires the ability to assess the credibility and authority of sources. It involves considering the expertise, reputation, and purpose of the author or organization, as well as the publication date and context of the information.

4. Information ethics

Information literacy includes understanding and practicing ethical and responsible information use. It involves respecting copyright laws, acknowledging sources through proper citation, and recognizing the ethical implications of information use and sharing.

Information ethics refer to the ethical considerations and principles that guide the responsible and ethical use, access, dissemination, and management of information. It involves examining the ethical implications and societal impact of information-related practices, technologies, and policies.

Key aspects of information ethics include:

a. Privacy and confidentiality

Respecting individuals' rights to privacy and safeguarding personal information. This includes the responsible collection, use, and storage of data, ensuring informed consent, and protecting sensitive information from unauthorized access or disclosure.

b. Intellectual property

Respecting and upholding intellectual property rights, including copyright, patents, and trademarks are quite important. Information ethics involves acknowledging and properly attributing the work of others, seeking permission for use when necessary, and avoiding plagiarism or infringement.

c. Access and equity

Promoting equal access to information and bridging the digital divide. Information ethics involves ensuring that information resources, technologies, and services are accessible to all individuals, regardless of socio-economic status, geographic location, or disabilities.

d. Accuracy and truthfulness

Upholding the principles of accuracy, truthfulness, and integrity in information dissemination plays an important role. Ethical information practices involve providing accurate and reliable information, avoiding misrepresentation or distortion, and correcting errors promptly.

e. Transparency and accountability

Being transparent and accountable for the collection, use, and handling of information is essential for success. This includes providing clear and understandable privacy policies, disclosing any potential conflicts of interest, and being accountable for the consequences of information-related decisions or actions.

f. Information security

Protecting information systems, networks, and data from unauthorized access, breaches, or cyber threats is the need of the hour. Information ethics involves implementing security measures, respecting user privacy and confidentiality, and taking steps to ensure the integrity and availability of information.

g. Ethical use of technology

One should consider the ethical implications of emerging technologies, such as artificial intelligence, big data analytics, and surveillance systems. Information ethics involves addressing issues related to bias, discrimination, privacy, and social impact when developing and implementing technology.

h. Social and cultural impact

One has to recognize social, cultural, and ethical implications of Information and Communication Technologies (ICTs) on individuals, communities, and society. Information ethics involves considering the broader societal implications of information practices, such as digital divide, information manipulation, or social media's influence on public discourse.

Information ethics guides individuals, organizations, policymakers, and information professionals in making ethical decisions and practices related to information. It ensures that ethical considerations are taken into account when handling information, engaging with technology, and shaping information policies and practices.

Promoting information ethics involves raising awareness, educating individuals about ethical issues, developing ethical guidelines and policies, fostering a culture of responsibility and integrity, and encouraging ethical decision-making in information-related contexts.

i. Information organization and management

Information literacy involves the skill of organizing and managing information effectively. It includes techniques for note-taking, citation management, and creating an organized system for storing and retrieving information.

j. Information synthesis and integration

Information literacy encompasses the ability to synthesize information from multiple sources, integrate diverse perspectives, and create new knowledge or insights. It involves critically analysing and connecting information to develop a comprehensive understanding of a topic.

k. Digital literacy

Information literacy is closely connected to digital literacy. It involves proficiency in using digital tools, technologies, and platforms for information seeking, evaluation, and communication. Digital literacy skills include online searching, data analysis, media literacy, and the ability to navigate and participate in online communities.

l. Lifelong learning

Information literacy emphasizes the importance of lifelong learning and the ability to adapt to new information and technologies. It involves continuously updating and expanding one's knowledge and skills to keep pace with evolving information landscapes.

Information literacy skills are essential in education, professional settings, and everyday life. They enable individuals to make informed decisions, engage in critical thinking, solve problems, and effectively communicate and share information with others. By becoming information literate, individuals can navigate the digital age with confidence and effectively contribute to society.

6. Digital Literacy

It is not computer literacy that we should be working on, but sort of human literacy. Computers have to become human-literate.

- Nicholas Negroponte

Digital literacy is an important professional skill in the 21st century. It involves an ability to use, understand, navigate and implement digital technology offline or online with the help of digital gadgets, tools and resources. In order to cope up with the present age, people now have to acquire digital skills and maintain the pace with the modern world. The people of this age have to be digitally lettered and capable to use digital equipment for engaging the self with digital information, communicate and collaborate and solve problems in the digital world. These days, digital literacy skills are the prerequisite for education, employment, enterprise, business, and participation in civic and over all personal development.

Digital literacy is being strongly promoted by educational institutions, private organizations, government and local bodies, by organizing training and awareness programmes. The main objective of digital literacy is to bridge the digital gap between the people and the modern world; similarly, it aims to empower an individual to deal technically and digitally with the world.

There are a few key components of digital literacy which include:

1. Basic Digital Skills

Computers, laptops, smart phones, palmtops are the digital devices which we use with the help of common computer programmes. In this century, we have to acquire basic digital skills in order to use these gadgets. We should know about the operating systems, web browsers, word processors, power point presentations, spreadsheets, file management, and use of different applications and programmes effectively.

2. Information literacy

Digital literacy includes the ability to understand and use digital information available online and offline in the digital form throughout the world. Information literacy provides an opportunity to search, evaluate, and analyse digital information. It also makes an individual capable to find relevant and credible data. Using online digital tools and platform also require a competence of analysing and interpreting the privacy of the data available and should be able to protect it from harmful attackers and programmes.

3. Communication and Collaboration

Communication and collaboration are essential skills for an individual. In this modern digital world, we communicate with the people all over the world by using different digital platforms like emails, social media, messaging systems, video conferencing, other online tools, etc. We collaborate with the people digitally now. So much of work is being done through digital ways.

4. Digital Creation and Creativity

Digital creation in the form of documents, designs, images, audios, videos, web content, software, digital codes and applications, etc. can be generated or created by putting in extra efforts with a polished knowledge of various tools of digital equipment. One has to develop the capacity to create, share and curate digital content.

5. Digital Citizenship and Digital Safety

Digital citizenship is a concept established in the modern time. In order to register any computer system, you have to generate your digital identity, log in to any website, you get your digital certification, downloading any information or data, you get your digital numerical order, whatever that you do with a digital platform, don't forget that you are provided with a digital identity. It shows that all of us are the digital citizens of Microsoft, Google, or any email or social media platform. This digital citizenship also encompasses some responsibility on our shoulders. We should be conscious of online security, safety, privacy protection, cyber security, copyrights, responsible behaviour on social media, and overall responsible use of digital resources.

In addition, one should be very careful about personal data protection, safety and security of your passwords, online financial transaction security, safe browsing and online threats, etc.

6. Adaptability and Digital Fluency

Being comfortable with the digital tools and gadgets is the demand of time. No one can keep himself or herself away from technology now. So, adapt technology and improve your fluency to effectively use it.

7. Digital Ethics

The impact of digital technology and digital tools is considerably deep. It has created a spiral grip on human mind. Right from a kid to an old person, no one can imagine life in the absence of internet, smart phones and electronic gadgets. This digital scenario has also imposed several principals and guidelines on the users. Being the user of internet facility and digital equipment, we should be very responsible and ethical user of internet and technology both.

8. Privacy and Data Protection

In this technological digital world, digital data protection and privacy of personal information has become the most important aspect. Data hackers, spywares, digital grey market are some of the issues and problems of this digital era. Every user should be careful of his personal information and safeguard it from the digital hackers. Protection of personal data and information has become personal responsibility of every user. A user should keep checking his digital accounts, its privacy, safety from hackers, should avoid giving permission to unauthorised apps and applications to peep into your personal details.

9. Online Security

Protecting your data and digital information from hackers and unauthorized users has become very crucial in the view of online security and protection against any online frauds. Every user should be cautious of cyber security. S/he should develop good habits of protecting personal information and data from data breaches, malware, cyber threats, and cyber-attacks. One should keep applications up-to-date and strong passwords in order to avoid malicious activities and phishing activities in your account.

10. Intellectual Property Rights

In the realm of digital world, it is crucial to respect one's intellectual property rights. The digital ethical values suggest that one has to give due credit to the original contributor for his/her creation and should never infringe into anybody's intellectual rights and avoid plagiarism and digital intellectual theft. By respecting the international copyrights, we actually support our ethics and ethical practice of obtaining permissions or giving citations whenever necessary and give credits to the intellectual copyright claimant.

11. Digital Footprints

Digital footprints and online reputation are quite important in this modern digital world. One should always remember that once something is created digitally and online; that can never be deleted forever. You may delete something for your convenience but your digital footprints remain forever in the data engines or memories of the respective service providing company. So, be ethical while using digital services and online tools for any purpose and don't forget that your digital presence, your reputation as a digital user makes a big matter. So, be cautious about sharing and using data, information, or creating anything online affect your digital footprints and digital presence.

12. Cyber bullying

While maintaining online interactions and communication on any social media or digital platform, one should be cautious of cyber bullying. It is unethical to engage in any kind of cyber bullying, harassment, or harmful behaviour online that can take you behind the bars. One should be ethically aware of his/her online / digital responsibility of being harmless and gentle regardless of geographic factors or socio-economic conditions.

13. Ethical artificial intelligence and automation

Artificial intelligence and automation are the fields which are in high demand and people are used to it. This sophisticated technology is considerably advanced and self-sufficient. Human mind has successfully given a mind to a machine also. When it comes to artificial intelligence and automation in AI GPT Chatbot and its functioning, this is beyond the imagination of a human mind. But at the same time, we, being the users, should be ethical enough to use such applications as a supporter not as a creator. Artificial intelligence systems are fair, transparent and unbiased in decision making, content writing and so on. Its algorithms are made accordingly, and that has ethical obligations as well.

14. Environmental Impact

New technology development and innovation should be made in the view to its impact on the environment. Environment friendly technological development is the need of the hour. A variety of digital equipment like computer hardware, mobiles, printers which we use today have a deep negative impact on the environment. So, e-waste management is our personal responsibility so that we will be able to keep this mother earth green.

These are the various key components of digital literacy that we should be always aware of. Being digitally lettered and digitally aware are two different things. But as a learned user of digital technology, one should always keep in mind about our friendliness with the mother earth.

7. Social Media

Engage, Enlighten, Encourage and especially just be yourself! Social media is a community effort, everyone is an asset.

-   Susan Cooper

Social media as a tool of communication and messaging has become very much popular in the 21st century. Since the smart phones have become a handy affordable tool of day-to-day affairs. The social media platforms like Facebook, Twitter, Instagram, LinkedIn, WhatsApp, Telegram, etc. are providing people worldwide messaging and communication platforms.

In the course of time, these platforms have been experienced extraordinary demand. As a result, the social media started influencing almost everything in our life. Social media is being used in different ways which shape business, culture, education, career, innovation, politics, society, and altogether human survival.

Social media are digital internet technology based interactive platforms which facilitate creation and sharing ideas, information, interests, and other expressions. The users get the benefit of being universally and virtually connected 24/7. In the modern time, these platforms have brought a revolution in digital and virtual communication and messaging system. Almost everybody in this world having digital exposure is well connected with the people around through social media platforms.

Social media platforms available for global messaging and networking can be divided into different categories. According to a few scholars, this division can be done based on the users and user type. The users using social media for social connectivity and networking are categorised as social networking media. Similarly, organizations using media platforms for circulating news are categorised as social news media. Then we have micro blogging and online forum sites for sharing views, information, opinions and so on.

A few important aspects of social media as universal and virtual tools for messaging and communication are discussed in the following sections:

1. Communication and Networking

Various social media platforms allow users to get connected virtually and communicate with the people around the world. The people can use these platforms for personal and business purposes. These social media platforms enable users to share and communicate ideas, messages, opinions, experiences, in real time and foster international networking and connectivity for the users across the globe for building virtual communities.

2. Information Sharing

Social media is informal type of communication and networking system. People use various platforms for sharing information which can be articles, videos, audios, news, commentaries, views, interests, and so on. It is crucial in the view of a user to verify and authenticate the information shared through media platforms. It is difficult to find out the source of information, its authenticity, and reliability. Many times, it is noticed that misinformation and unreliable content have been shared in order to influence the opinion of the users.

3. Personal Branding

In order to create virtual presence of an individual or business establishment, users use various social media platforms for branding of the self or a product. Social media platforms allow users to project their expertise, knowledge, achievement, skills, and other abilities at a large level among their contacts and outside contacts worldwide. The users use such facilities for personal or business purposes.

4. Privacy and Security

In this digital world, privacy and security of personal data and information has become a prime responsibility of a digital platform user. Social media encourage users to share almost everything that the people want to share. In fact, the users should be very careful while sharing their personal information online. Similarly, the users are expected to keep checking their privacy settings of their social media accounts and kind of permissions given to the social media corporation for accessing their accounts. Protection of privacy, data and security has become a personal commitment now.

5. Digital Etiquettes

Social media have the global presence and the users belong to different cultures, civilizations, countries, religions, ethnicity, language backgrounds and so on. The users also have their own preferences, opinions, political choices, likes and dislikes, so, every user of social media should feel a social responsibility of respecting others' opinions, religious sentiments, political preferences, cultural values, social concerns and status and so on. Digital etiquettes teach us being mindful about all these concerns of every individual user so that harmonious communication and messaging will take place all over the world.

Using social media for networking and messaging also imposes digital responsibility on the shoulder of every user. In order to reap the benefits of technology and social media, we the users are expected to be cautious of potential risks and drawbacks of digital platforms. So, upgrading the digital literacy, security of data and personal information and justified use of social media for the upliftment of human beings by getting virtually connected with the people all over the world should be the major motive behind adapting these platforms.

8. Global Awareness

You are never alone. You are eternally connected with everyone.

-   Amit Ray

Global awareness is one of the most important professional skills in the 21ˢᵗ century. This skill involves understanding and appreciating the interconnectedness of the entire world. It recognises its diverse perspectives, global issues, and so on. Hence having global awareness is considered as desperately required. In order to understand the global issues and its interconnectedness, an individual should have the knowledge of various cultures, languages, ethnic values, traditions, political, environmental, social and economic status and so on. This global awareness skill enables an individual to look at global issues with all possible perspectives and address the problems with critical and innovative ways.

These days, India has come forward with global leadership and inculcated the principle of 'Vasudhaiva Kutumbakam' which mainly promotes the concept of the entire world as a single family and religion of humanity. In addition, we keep talking about the concept 'think locally and act globally'. This actually provides us a micro level understanding of the needs and problems at a local level and the new ways of addressing the issues to serve them globally.

There are a few important aspects of global awareness which are discussed in the following sections:

1. Interconnectedness

The digital revolution and internet technology has established the concept of 'global village'. As we are digitally connected by all means, aviation industry transporting people all around in a few hours, everything that happens has immediate effect on the other region of the world. This interconnectedness has made us interdependent. Now no one can think of living alone. In fact, no one can be alone at all. We are the integral part and parcel of this world. We are eternally connected with one another forever. This creates global awareness which involves recognising our interconnectedness in the form of economy, cultures, societies, languages, traditions, customs, attires, cuisine and so on.

2. Cultural Competence

Today's face of the earth is – we are living in a global village where we experience multicultural atmosphere. Different cultures have essentially different ethics, values, perspectives, customs, traditions, practices and so on. It basically involves being tolerant, peaceful, open-minded, and respectful towards other people even though we belong to diverse backgrounds and belonging. As a whole, one should remember that one has to recognize and respect this cultural diversity and accept this multi-cultural face of the world where a human being should be respected with all his heritage, culture and belongings.

3. Global Issues and Challenges

The world is facing many problems and challenges. There are many global issues like, climate, change, poverty, global warming, inequality, migration, human rights, human trafficking, international conflicts, wars and so on. We being the citizens of this earth have a responsibility to tackle with these global issues and challenges. Addressing these challenges need a holistic perspective and professional dealing. Creating global awareness about the causes, consequences, problems, solutions, and so on is desperately required now. If we don't pay attention to these challenges, then our future generations will face the acute consequences.

4. Global Citizenship

Being a citizen of a country, we have a few duties to perform them, then we claim our constitutional rights. Being a global citizen, we too have a similar role to perform for keeping this earth healthy and sound. We need to embrace a sense of responsibility and engagement towards global issues and challenges. Once we start believing in the principle of 'Vasudhaiva Kutumbakam' which is the religion of humanity; obviously we will advocate social issues, problems, and challenges at large and put in efforts to address them.

5. Global Communication

It is the demand of the present time that we should engage in very effective global communication and collaboration across multi-cultures, languages, geographical boundaries, and other global aspects. Inter-cultural and cross-cultural communication can create international platform for conducive global relationship. Today technology has provided several tools and platforms for successful and effective global communication; as a result, issues related to cross-culture have been minimised in the course of time. The multinational business corporations, aviation, migration and a few more factors have considerably contributed to global communication.

6. Environmental Sustainability

The environmental issues like global warming, deforestation, scarcity of water, pollution, climate change have already been ringing alarm bells. Unless we become aware of these problems and address them skilfully; the problem will remain to be our heritage to the next generation. So, we have to recognize the importance of environmental stewardship and understanding the global impact of human activities on the environment. We, the advanced human beings, should develop new technologies which are sustainable to environment and create awareness about biodiversity, natural resource management, pro-nature activities, and agriculture and industrial development.

7.   Human Rights and Social Justice

Human beings live in a society and have cultures and civilizations. So, understanding human problems related to basic human rights, social justice, human trafficking, child abuse, equality, gender discrimination are the top priorities now. Global awareness basically looks into these issues and is expected to offer solutions to these problems wherever they are happening irrespective region, country, society, or religion.

8.   Media Literacy

In the modern era, electronic and print media play a very crucial role in order to create perception of people about certain issues or problems. Global awareness also includes understanding media bias, misinformation, and narratives. The responsible media will have a balanced and just approach to particular problem, but in these days, it is experienced that the international media has been strongly influencing on shaping global narratives and public opinions. So, the global citizens should understand all these happenings around and evaluate and interpret the global news, information and media content logically.

9.   Global Economic Literacy

The presence of multinational corporations and their business at international level has created a need of global economic literacy. It involves understanding the interconnected global economy and multinational businesses. People should have knowledge of international laws, trade, global market, economic systems, world trade organization and its functioning, international monetary fund organizations, etc. In order to live in this mercantile world, one should have a better understanding of all the economic system around.

Developing global awareness is an important professional skill in the 21st century. This awareness basically promotes empathy towards the emotional issues such as child labour, gender discrimination, inequality, etc. Similarly, it makes us aware of other global challenges such as global warming, changing climate, pollution, etc. which are raising a question about the survival of human generations in the days to come.

9. Adaptability and Flexibility

There can be no life without change, and to be afraid of what is different or unfamiliar is to be afraid of life.

- Theodore Roosevelt

Adaptability and flexibility are the essential professional skills in the 21ˢᵗ century. These skills involve an ability to get adjusted to new situations, embrace change and thrive in dynamic environment. In this rapidly changing time, these skills enable an individual to learn, unlearn and relearn in order to give a positive response to the changing circumstances.

There are a few aspects which are the necessary for developing adaptability and flexibility skills:

1. Accepting Change

Generally, open-minded people quickly adapt to the changes taking place around. It shows their flexibility to acquire changes in professional and personal life. The professionals those who possess these skills never resist to new ideas and upgradation in life. While working in an organization, several changes do take place in terms of work processes, technology, environment, teams and human resources, etc. So, always be open to embrace change in personal and professional life.

2. Learning Agility

Human beings are always in the process of learning new things every day. The people with adaptability and flexibility skills have a positive mindset to learn new skills, acquire new knowledge and information, and update themselves to the tunes of the current time. It shows the liveliness of an individual to learning ability.

3. Resilience

Personal and professional life is always full of challenges, ups and downs. In order to cope up with these adversities in life, one should have resilience to face setbacks, adversities and challenges in life. The professionals having this skill can easily adjust to the circumstances around and maintain a positive attitude to face the obstacles.

4. Versatility

Having a versatile personality is an asset to adaptability and flexibility. It involves being versatile and adaptable in various roles and contexts. Individuals with these skills can switch between different tasks, projects, and responsibilities with ease, and can work effectively in diverse teams and environments.

5. Interpersonal Adaptability

Adaptability and flexibility include the ability to work well with diverse individuals and adapt one's communication and collaboration style to different personalities and cultural contexts.

6. Time Management

Adaptability and flexibility require effective time management skills. Individuals with these skills can prioritize tasks, manage competing demands, and adjust their plans as new priorities or deadlines arise.

7. Innovation and Creativity

Adaptability and flexibility involve fostering an innovative and creative mindset. Individuals with these skills are open to exploring new ideas, experimenting with different approaches, and thinking outside the box to find innovative solutions.

8. Agility in Technology

Adaptability and flexibility encompass the ability to adapt to new technologies and digital tools. Individuals with these skills can quickly learn and utilize new software, platforms, and digital workflows to enhance their productivity and effectiveness.

9. Cultural Adaptability

Adaptability and flexibility involve being culturally adaptable and sensitive to different cultural norms and practices. Individuals with these skills can navigate cross-cultural interactions, work effectively in multicultural teams, and adjust their behaviours and communication styles accordingly.

Developing adaptability and flexibility requires a willingness to embrace change, a growth mindset, and a commitment to ongoing learning and self-improvement. These skills empower individuals to thrive in dynamic and uncertain environments, embrace new opportunities, and successfully navigate the complexities of the 21st century.

10. Initiative and Entrepreneurship

Entrepreneurship is about turning what excites in life in to capital, so that you can do more of it and move forward with it.

- Richard Branson

Initiative and entrepreneurship are vital professional skills required in the 21st century. These two skills encourage an individual to be proactive about taking action, identifying opportunities, and creating value. These skills allow an individual to be innovative thinkers, agents of change, and self-starter as well.

A few key aspects of initiative and entrepreneurship are as follows:

1. Pro-activeness

The word initiative indicates that it involves positive and active involvement of an individual by taking a lead and initiating an action. The individuals who are self-motivated take up the responsibility and prove their enterprising nature. They keep on seeking new opportunities for growth and improvement.

2. Identifying Opportunities

Initiative and entrepreneurship always demand from an individual the ability to identify the upcoming opportunities and capitalize the same for the benefit of the organization. The employees or entrepreneurs with these skills do have keen observations of the happenings around. Their sense of observations and being alert for identifying the trends make them capable to identify the gaps in the market and the probable areas for improvement.

3. Creativity and Innovation

As discussed earlier, creativity and innovation are the next steps towards perfection. Initiative and entrepreneurship encompass creativity and innovativeness. There is a wide scope for the individuals having these skills. The people having these skills are open to learning something new, they think out of the box, they take challenges and convert them into opportunities, their ability of critical thinking and innovativeness provide a different solution to certain problem, and similarly they have novel ideas.

4. Risk Taking

The willingness of an individual to take risk shows his or her ability to take initiatives and enterprising nature. In any business or enterprise, the risk-taking ability becomes the deciding factor for the success of the organization. The people with risk taking ability are aware of the uncertainty of the future happenings but they are ready to face failure and setbacks. In business, it is said that bigger risk leads to bigger profit.

5. Resourcefulness

In order to achieve goals in personal or professional life, resources make a big difference. The resources are of three types - human resources, natural resources and capital resources. Every organization should keep in mind that being resourceful means being resourceful in all these three areas. Expertise in all these can make a big difference to achieve the goals.

6. Self-direction

Initiative and entrepreneurship engage in self-direction, self-motivation and autonomy of work. The people with these skills are highly energetic and proactive. They have their own targets, goals, and strategies to achieve these goals. Such people do not like over monitoring and supervision. They prefer autonomy in work and they are confident of their approach and results.

7. Problem-Solving

The chapter titled, *Critical Thinking and Problem Solving*, a detailed discussion has been done. Problems do take place frequently. Looking at it with a different perspective and the way it is being addressed decides the success. Initiative and entrepreneurship include strong problem-solving skills. One has to identify the problem, critically think about it in order to find a suitable solution. So, the approach of an individual should be not to dig up the problem but to find a solution for it.

8. Networking and Relationship Building

Initiative and entrepreneurship involve networking and building relationships. In any organization, these skills are considered important and every individual must have. The people having these skills develop strong teams, collaborate with others, and negotiate with other people and organizations effectively, use different resources as needed through their networking ability.

9. Business insight

Business insight is necessary for every individual for effective initiation and succeeded entrepreneurship. Individuals who possess these skills have better understanding of the business, market dynamics, financial management, and other important aspects of business.

10. Adaptability and Resilience

Initiative and entrepreneurship also involve adaptability and resilience. Business environment shows uncertainty of results; hence every individual should have the skills of adaptability and must be flexible in approach while dealing with people and issues. The ultimate goal should be to succeed in every attempt irrespective of uncertainty.

Finally, it can be said that initiative and entrepreneurship involve a culture of developing a mindset to be proactive, creative and innovative, be open to learn new things, and have passion for growth and value creation. With these skills an individual can stand better to create his/her own presence as a professional of the present century.

11. Emotional Intelligence

Emotional maturity occurs when we can express our true feelings, without need for reciprocation, validation, appreciation or trepidation. Our feelings become companions rather than enemies.

- *L.A. Askew*

Emotional Intelligence (EI) is one of the important professional skills of the 21ˢᵗ century. This skill employs the ability of an individual to recognize, understand and manage emotions of the self and others as well. It also includes personal and social emotional competencies which contribute to relationship building, social involvement, empathy and effective interpersonal communication.

The key factors related to emotional intelligence are discussed below:

1. Self-awareness

'Know thyself' is a very famous phrase in personality development. Similarly, self-awareness allows an individual to identify his or her own self. Understanding the self means recognizing one's own emotions, strengths, weaknesses, values, ideology, and status which allows an individual to assess own emotions, thoughts, behaviours, interpersonal skills, and attitude accurately. These factors do affect others in different ways.

2. Self-regulation

Effectively managing one's own self is considered quite crucial in emotional intelligence. The individuals who have strong self-regulation skills can control their emotions, impulses, stress, and pro-act to the situations around. They always demonstrate discipline, flexibility, patience, and face any challenging situation with a composed attitude and cool mind.

3. Empathy

Showing empathy is an integral aspect of emotional intelligence. An individual having the ability to understand and share others' emotions and feelings with a lot of personal attachment shows his or her emphatic attitude. Listening to others attentively, demonstrating sensitivity to the perspectives of others, giving others emotional support, putting himself into others shoes, enhancing interpersonal relations, being emphatic for others are some of the features of an individual who is very cautious of others and shows his/her emotional concern.

4. Social Skills

As a philosopher said, man is a social animal and prefers to live in a community of men and women. It indicates that every human being loves the company of other people. Emotional intelligence also encompasses and demands strong social skills in order to build and maintain a strong bond of relationship. Being empathic also shows a sign of being social. In addition, one should make an attempt to be an active listener, polite respondent, skilled problem shooter, and most importantly show concern for others. These skills will help an individual to communicate effectively, solve the problems skilfully, and mobilize the people amicably.

5. Relationship Management

Managing people with good relations is one of the emotional intelligence skills. An individual should have ability to maintain and nurture relationships and seek best of their support and cooperation for the benefit of the society and organization. Individuals with strong relationship management skills can build strong teams, extract best of the individual, navigate social dynamics, motivate and inspire people, foster positive environment, and so on.

6. Emotional Awareness

Emotional awareness of the people around is equally important as self-awareness. The people with self-awareness can understand other people comfortably and easily. Understanding other people's behaviour based on their dealings, body language, facial expressions, optical glances, non-verbal cues, and gestures make an individual socially and emotionally aware of others. Such people can build a rapport with others and keep the people together emotionally.

7. Conflict Resolution

Conflicts are inevitable in personal and professional life. Emotional intelligence also encompasses the ability to have an insight into a conflict and addressing the same with an acceptable resolution. Dealing with a conflict needs basic understanding of the ground reality, critical thinking with an aptitude to solve the issue with a win-win solution, proactively conveying the resolution and manage emotions during the conflicts.

8. Emotional Resilience

Emotional resilience is an important aspect of emotional intelligence. It is an ability of an individual to bounce back from setbacks and adversities in personal and professional life. Unless a professional is flexible in his approach, s/he will not be able to adapt to changes, stress, and maintain a new outlook to life. The people with emotional resilience are open-minded and they learn from setbacks, maintain a sense of optimism, and they quickly recover from the failures.

9. Emotional Regulation

Helping others in regulating their emotions is a necessary emotional intelligence in the present time. In this world of complexities, dissociation and isolation, people need someone who can extend emotional support and offer them constructive feedback by helping them to regulate their emotions in challenging situations.

10. Leadership

It is the leader who can make a big difference in the success of a team. Emotional intelligence is closely linked to leadership skills. A good leader handles emotions of the self and others skilfully for the benefit of all. The leaders with emotional intelligence can build strong teams, can handle complex issues, solve difficult problems, and navigate social and professional dynamics. Such leaders are self-aware, emphatic, understand and manage others emotionally, and most importantly they extract the best of all for the benefit of the organization.

These are the ten crucial factors of emotional intelligence. It is the emotional intelligence that can make an individual emphatic, self-directed, proactive, and highly motivated. An individual with emotional intelligence is also effective in communication, relationship building, human resource management, and so on. Hence this skill has got exceptional importance in professional life of the 21st century.

12. Leadership and Responsibility

A leader is one who knows the way, goes the way, and shows the way.

-   John C. Maxwell

Leadership and responsibility are the crucial professional skills in the 21ˢᵗ century. These skills include leading, guiding and influencing others in order to achieve a common goal. Leadership and responsibility automatically impose accountability on the part of the individual who is performing the role. These skills are important for every professional in the present time. Leading a team effectively, making/taking ethical decisions, achieving common goals, and contributing to the society make the professional perfect by all means.

The points given below will provide the intrinsic inputs about leadership and responsibility skills:

1.   Vision and Goal Setting

Leadership in due course carries responsibility. A leader should have a clear vision, and a compelling goal to achieve. The vision and goal inspire others to take a call and move forward along with the leader. The leader should know what to do, how to do and when to do. S/He should be a guiding source and example for others and a collaborator for every action. S/He should move on with a plan and have a strategy with an objective.

2.   Decision Making

Leadership skill demands an ability of an individual to take right decision at the right time. The professional ethics, proper understanding of the matter, relevant information, analytical skills, diverse perspectives, and values have collective influence on the process of decision making. A leader is expected to be firm, clear and decisive in his/her approach.

3. Communication

Communication is a key to success in the present scenario. Leadership and responsibility skills need strong command over communication skills. Having the knowledge of multiple languages enables an individual to effectively communicate with the members of a team, clients, and so on. A leader having effective communication skills can strongly convey the vision, goals, and mission of the organization and team. Active listening, speaking, reading and writing along with good knowledge of grammar makes an individual effective in communication skills.

4. Motivation

A leader should be a performer, guide, mentor, and an effective motivator. S/He should keep inspiring the members of his/her team and should always think of making other leaders than the followers. A word of motivation, accelerate a follower and give him or her proper direction to perform some action. So, a leader should influence each member of his/her team in order to make them proactive for achieving the goals of the organization. A leader should assign a task, pursuit the matter, offer suggestions, give a proper guidance, recognize talent, and appreciate a task master.

5. Team Building

'Together everyone achieves more' is fundamental principle of team building. Leadership skill includes the ability to foster team building and collaboration in order to achieve organizational goals. Leaders having diverse perspectives can collaborate and build a team. The days are gone to work in isolation, every task assigned to an individual need collaboration and support of others. In the absence of a leader, team cannot function as one entity. In addition, a leader should be always positive to empower his/her team members and provide them opportunities for growth and development in career.

6. Ethical Behaviour

A successful leader should have own ethical values and an ethical stance to adhere the same in professional life. In addition, a leader should always behave with a sense of responsibility, honesty, integrity, transparency and should take responsibility for the decisions taken. S/He should feel accountable for all – s/he should admit mistakes, take initiative, face hindrances, solve problems, support his/her teammates, and so on. It is the ethical identity of a leader who gains respect for his/her deeds and action.

7. Adaptability and Flexibility

Adaptability and flexibility are the most important skills which a leader must have. Open-mindedness to learn and adapt new things should be on the agenda of a good leader. In addition, s/he should be flexible in approach while dealing with any situation, issue or a problem. This openness for adaptability and flexibility allows a leader to navigate changing situations, address problems methodically, overcome obstacles, maintain calmness of mind, and be composed in adverse situations.

8. Social and Cultural Awareness

Being an integral part of culture and society, a leader should have a sensibility and empathy for social and cultural issues. The proper understanding of cultural and social dynamics provides an opportunity to a leader to develop his attitude to respect the people of diverse cultures, languages, ethnicity, and religions. This approach promotes fairness, inclusivity, equality, and team spirit.

9. Empathy

Leaders are expected to have empathy for the people working in the team. In general, it is observed that the leaders show genuine concern and care for their colleagues and co-workers. This empathy enhances the level of building amicable relationship, genuine care and concern, vote of trust for one another and favourable atmosphere. Such leaders manage their emotions and handle the conflict logically with empathy and diplomacy.

10. Accountability and Integrity

Accountability and integrity have to be demonstrated by the leaders by setting an example of actions. Leaders should take responsibility for their actions, decisions, and admit mistakes. They are expected to be ethical and promote a culture of trust and transparency.

11. Managerial Skills

Managerial skills refer to one's competence of handling multiple things at a time in a systematic way. A systematic management of man power, resources, and processes within the organization are expected to be done by the leaders. These skills are necessary for every individual who has occupied managerial position in the hierarchy of an organization. The manager knows the objectives, goals and mission of the organization and has a plan to execute in order to attain the goals.

Planning and organizing resources, strategically solving the problems, resolving conflicts, finance management, etc. are some of the important deals which the leader or the manager is expected to perform for the success of the organization.

These are some of the intrinsic inputs about leadership and responsibility skills. In order to be an effective and influencing leader, one must acquire these skills and hone the same till perfection. In a presentation delivered by Mr. Mulidhar Koteshwar for HRDC Goa, he talked about ten leadership principles which are given bellow:

Ten LEADERSHIP Principles

Leading by example

Enable leaders, not followers

Alertness during challenges

Delegation to help achieve more

Enable control to relevant people

Respect to be commanded, not to be demanded

Solve problems head on, don't be an ostrich

Head Vs. Heart - balance the need of the hour with personal pulls

Inspire and care for the team

Present moment – no judgement including the self.

If someone could remember these principles of LEADERSHIP, it will be helpful for a budding leader to implement the same in his or her career and achieve success.

13. Communication Skills

To effectively communicate, we must realize that we are all different in the way we perceive the world and use this understanding as a guide to our communication with others.

-   Tony Robbins

Communication skills are success mantra today. LSRW skills refer to the four components of effective communication: Listening, Speaking, Reading, and Writing. These are the four fundamental skills for effective communication in personal, academic and professional life. An individual should have command over a language in addition, one should develop these four skills for establishing an effective communication. In this global world, English has established itself as a language for international communication. Hence, one should master English and the four LSRW skills in this language in order to maintain a pace with the rest of the world.

LSRW skills can be categorised into two categories: Receptive Skills and Productive Skills. Listening and reading are the receptive skills whereas speaking and writing are the productive skills. The following sections deal with these four skills categorically in detail along with the importance of non-verbal communication.

1. Listening

Listening is a receptive skill which demands receiving sound signals from different sources around. Listening involves actively listening, receiving and interpreting verbal and non-verbal messages from others. It also requires focused attention to the speaker or the source of the sounds in order to decode the message properly and understand it in the same context. Similarly, listener should give attention to the thoughts, emotions, tone, intonations, stressing pattern, use of words, and sentence structure of the language being used by the speaker. Most importantly, a listener is expected to be very cautious while listening to others about their body language, optical glances, non-verbal cues, gestures and movements. This kinesics communicates a lot and adds on certain meaning to the verbal context a speaker speaks. In addition, a listener should be attentive, maintain eye contact with the speaker, avoid internal and external distractions, and clarify doubts by asking questions to the speaker.

Tips for effective listening

> ➢ Pay full attention to the speaker and practice active listening

> ➢ Remember that you should listen to the people not hear

> ➢ Allow the speaker to finish before asking any doubt and never interrupt

> ➢ Take running notes which helps you to retain important points and information

> ➢ Use non-verbal cues such as nodding head, proper posture, focused attention and showing interest in the context of the speaker.

By following these tips one can improve listening skill. Always remember an effective listener proves to be an effective speaker. Listening and Speaking are the interconnected and interdependent skills. You cannot imagine the presence of one in the absence of the other. A speaker will not speak unless there is a listener and vice versa.

2. Speaking

Speaking is a productive skill because a speaker produces different sounds as the language context. This skill demands an individual's ability to produce acceptable sound in a particular language. Speaking skill involves expressing thoughts, ideas, experiences, observations, knowledge, and information to the listeners clearly and effectively in a language which both listener and speaker understand. This skill also requires effective verbal communication skills, vocabulary, command over grammar, proper pronunciation, effective speaking/delivery style, appropriate tone, knowledge of stressing pattern, and most important is to understand the pulse of the listeners.

Tips for effective speaking

> Practice articulating your thoughts, ideas, observations and experiences aloud

> Pay attention to your pronunciation, stressing pattern, tone groups and speech

> Be careful about the use of vocabulary and be appropriate

> Use suitable language in a proper tone

> Organise your ideas and thoughts logically

> Use examples, quotations, visuals, etc. for effective speaking

> Try to understand the pulse of the listeners and make an attempt to seek feedback from others

> Maintain proper body posture

> Use non-verbal cues and body movements properly

> Never do the things which you don't like as a listener.

In order to develop effective speaking skills, these tips will certainly help an individual. An individual should always remember that your constant practice to share your ideas and thoughts at different formal and informal platforms will help you to hone and improve your skills. So, don't forget, practice makes man perfect.

3. Reading

Reading is a receptive skill that makes man knowledgeable. This skill involves comprehension form in written or printed texts, content on the screen, any image, flex, advertisement, poster, etc. The ability of an individual to interpret and analyse the read content decides the success of reading. Reading skill includes understanding the author's perspective by interpreting key points, critically analysing the content and information provided. Effective reading enables an individual to gather and seek correct information without differing with the subject matter. The vocabulary power, good knowledge of grammar of the respective language, habit of keen and careful reading, and a better understanding across various subjects can make an individual good at reading.

Depending on the need of the reader, s/he can opt for the kind of reading like scanning, skimming, intensive and extensive reading. In order to understand the gist of the content, we prefer skimming. To find out a particular piece of information, we prefer scanning. For accurate reading and understanding, we go for intensive reading and the extensive reading is used for pleasure, entertainment and general understanding. So, depending upon the need of the reader, one can opt for the right kind of approach and be a voracious reader.

Tips for effective reading

> Develop a habit of reading good books or content

> Build vocabulary and comprehension

> Begin with a simple text and gradually move on to complex books and content

> Take running notes in order to understand and remember the key points

> Write short summaries to reflect on the read content

> Practice skimming and scanning as needed

> Practice intensive and extensive reading also

> Discuss and analyse the content in order to deepen your understanding.

These tips will help an individual to deepen the understanding of the content or text processed during the course of reading.

4. Writing

Writing is a productive skill. There is a famous sentence in English- 'Writing makes a man perfect'. Writing skill is considered to the most difficult skill among the LSRW. It involves expressing ideas, thoughts, emotions, feelings, experiences, observations in structured written form. In order to hone this skill, it demands command over grammar, spellings, vocabulary, and sentence structures. Effective writing enables an individual with clear communication, persuasive arguments, and a platform for conveying information and messages.

Tips for effective writing

- Enhance your vocabulary to provide diversity in writing

- Grasp different styles of writing

- Practice writing regularly and write at least a few short pieces of texts

- Plan your writing and make an outline before you start

- Organize your thoughts and structure them logically

- Use clear and concise language, avoid jargons and ambiguity

- Always proof read your content before finalising the document

- Edit the draft for a couple of times till you feel convinced

- Be careful about grammar, structure, spellings, clarity of thoughts and expressions.

Remember that writing is considered to be the most difficult skill. It involves all senses of human body. So, be focused, diverse, consistent and take feedback about your content. If possible, join some writing group to enhance your creativity and spontaneity of writing. Extensive reading can provide better understand of effective writing also. So reading is equally important for a creative writer. If you want to improve your writing skill, first improve your reading skill and then reflect on it in written context.

LSRW are the most crucial and essential skills for every professional in the 21st century. In this modern era, English has got so much importance and it has become the language for global communication and the language for respectable survival. So, no one can take the risk of ignoring this language today. In order to be capable and efficient in language skills, one has to develop and sharpen LSRW skills.

5. Non-Verbal Communication

LSRW skills aligned with non-verbal communication skills can take an individual to next level of proficiency in language competence. The following section deals with non-verbal communication.

Non-verbal communication refers to the communication, transmission and reception of messages without the use of verbal words or production of sounds. It involves facial expressions, gestures, body language, eye contact and optical glances, tone of voice, non-verbal cues, attitudes, emotions and feelings and so on. In the chapter *Collaboration and Communication*, we dealt with non-verbal communication in a nutshell. Here an attempt will be made to look into all the aspects of non-verbal communication in detail.

Non-verbal communication plays an important role in the entire process of interpersonal communication and it allows an individual to convey information to the audience which complements or contradict to the spoken words.

The following sections will provide comprehensive information about key aspects of non-verbal communication:

a. Facial expressions

One can hide feelings and emotions by pronouncing words, but no one can hide facial expressions. Facial expressions are more talkative than words. In English, there is a famous proverb, "action speaks louder than words". So, human expressions like smiles, frowns, eye brows, facial movements, emotions of agreement, disagreement, happiness, sorrow, sadness, surprise, anger, etc. are the most powerful forms of non-verbal communication in the entire process.

b. Body language

Body language includes postures (standing, sitting, moving, relaxing, defensive), facial gestures, personal attitudes, intentions, emotions, and so on. An effective speaker is always very much conscious of body language. Body language enables a speaker to convey his/her verbal message strongly. In fact, body language in any form supports the speaker to make his/her verbal interaction more convincing and acceptable.

c. Optical contact

Eye contact plays a very significant role in the process of successful communication. One can deceive the whole world by spoken or written words, but your eyes will always tell the truth. Eye contact demonstrates interest, attentiveness, sincerity, and confidence of an individual. In different countries, we find various cultural norms, preferences and eye contacts in different situations. But altogether, it is observed that eyes are more talkative than body and words. Complex feelings and emotions like anger, disagreement, love, passion, hate, malice, and so on are clearly visible in the eyes of an individual.

d. Tone of voice

Tone of voice makes a big difference in the entire process of communication. Different tones have different meanings. Tone of voice which includes pitch, volume, intonation and rhythm convey emotions, attitudes and focus on a particular word or thought. A loud voice with aggressive tone may suggest anger and frustration, a calm and soothing tone may indicate reassurance, change in high and low may indicate the level of importance of particular thought. Change in intonation groups like falling, rising, rising-falling and falling-rising have their own importance and meaning.

e. Personal space

The distance maintained between individual and audience during the interactions also communicate diverse levels of comfort, formality, or intimacy. A speaker has to maintain own proximity which gives some comfort to an individual. In cross-cultural communication, we learned that different cultures have dissimilar preferences of proximity and personal space.

f. Touch

Touch is also an important aspect of non-verbal communication. Touch conveys diverse meanings like affection, love, passion, comfort, support, dominance, and so on. Different cultures have vivid norms and practices related to touch and relationship between individuals.

g. Appearance

In the professional life, personal grooming and overall appearance carry lot of importance. An individual should be aware of his/her professional identity while maintaining personal grooming, clothing sense, and so on. Personal maintenance by all means indicates one's identity, social status, economic status, and professionalism. It also indicates your impression on others by your appearance and perceptions of life.

h. Silence

Silence is considered to be a biggest weapon. But in the context of non-verbal communication, silence and pauses have a considerable value. Silence and pauses indicate thoughtfulness, hesitation, need for reflection, agreement or disagreement. Silence can have its own situational interpretation.

In addition to these aspects of non-verbal communication, the colours, signals, images, also contribute to the process of effective communication. In a nutshell, one can say that LSRW skills provided with non-verbal communication skills support an individual to effectively communicate with the world around.

14. Presentation Skills

The success of your presentation will be judged not by the knowledge you send but by what the listener receives.

- *Lilly Walters*

Presentations skills are crucial in the view to deliver information, ideas, proposals, research, academic and non-academic topics effectively in a clear, engaging and persuasive manner. Strong presentation skills help an individual to convey his/her message effectively in formal or informal situations and leave a lasting impression in the audience.

There are different types of presentations which are commonly used by individuals in various contexts. A few identified types of presentations are given below:

1. Informative Presentation

The objective of informative presentation is to enhance the level of knowledge of the expected audience about a particular topic or subject matter. Such kind of presentation mainly focuses on providing some information or to educate the audience about the assigned topic.

2. Persuasive Presentation

The objective of this type of prtesentation is to convince the audience to adopt a certain viewpoint and take a specific action or change behaviour. This presentation makes an attempt to change belief of the audience by making arguments, providing evidence, or making an emotional appeal to persuade the audience.

3. Sales Presentation

Sales presentations are used in order to promote a product, service or idea. The objective of this kind of presentation is to describe and highlight the benefits, features, and utility value of a product, service or idea for the expected buyers, consumers, or customers. Such presentations make an attempt to persuade the expected audience to buy a product or utilize a service.

4. Instructional Presentation

Instructional presentations are focused and always target specific skill set, procedures, or concepts to be inculcated among the expected audience. This type of presentation provides training on specific topic, skill set, procedure, concept, etc. in order to hone the same among the audience. It can be in the form of instructions, demonstrations, practical, etc. Hence, this type of presentation is also called Training presentation.

5. Demonstration Presentation

Demonstration presentation typically provides a live demonstration of a product or process or concept by highlighting the salient features, functions, steps, and procedures of a product or process. The demonstration educates the audience about the product, process or concept thoroughly.

6. Pitch Presentation

In order to secure some support, funding or collaboration, such presentations are arranged in which a new business idea, project, or start-up is presented to the potential investor, partner, or stakeholder. The main goal of pitch presentation is to convince the expected audience for thinking in favour of the presenter.

7. Panel Discussion

In order to understand a particular subject or topic comprehensively, panel discussions are conducted in which experts or panellists invited present their views, observations, experiences and thoughts on a particular topic or subject and try to convince their audience. Such presentations or discussions are moderated to provide a better understanding to the audience.

8. Conference Presentation

Professional conferences, seminars, symposiums, academic deliberations, professional talks are being organized in order to address a particular subject or a few subtopics related. Participants, delegates, experts, resource persons actively contribute in such events and share their research findings, innovative ideas, industry insights to the audience.

9. Motivational Presentation

Motivational presentations are organized to motivate, inspire and uplift the expected audience. The presenter shares stories, personal experiences, inspirational messages, motivational quotations, positive aspirations, standards and high morals to encourage audience to follow the same in their lives. The objective of such presentations is to bring certain change in the mind and psychology of the audience to bring them to certain path of values and morals.

10. Webinar Presentation

Webinar presentations are also called virtual or online presentations. The objective of such presentation is to digitally bring together different professionals or people who are geographically away from one another and assemble them virtually in a webinar. Webinars were extensively used during the covid-19 pandemic. In order to organize webinars, we need internet connectivity along with an unanimously decided webinar platform like Zoom, Google Meet, Microsoft Teams, etc. It also demands certain digital literacy to use various functions of such platforms.

These are various types of presentations which we have categorised based on the objectives and its usefulness. To be an effective speaker in a presentation of any kind, one should have certain skills especially effective communication skills along with a good command over the language in which presentation is being made.

There are a few tips to improve presentation skills, they are as follows:

a. Know your audience

A good speaker always makes an effort to understand the pulse of his/her audience. It is the audience who decides the success or failure of the presentation. A speaker should find out the needs, interest and knowledge level of the audience so that s/he will be able to deliver his/her presentation accordingly. A professional speaker very particularly addresses these concerns and engages the audience effectively.

b. Plan and structure your presentation

A good speaker personally chalks out his plan of the presentation and systematically structures the entire presentation. A professional speaker begins with an attention-grabbing introduction, provides a clear outline of his talk and concludes with a concise summary. His/her presentation is always provided with headings, bulleted points, visual aids and utmost clarity and comprehension.

c. Use of visual aids

A successful speaker prefers to provide some visual aids to his audience so that they understand and focus during the actual presentation. Visual aids actually support both – the presenter as well as the audience. While using visual aids, the speaker should limit his power point slides to a justified number. Slides allow the audience to focus the presentation and take important notes as needed. Visual aids enhance the level of understanding of the audience and give an opportunity to the speaker to maintain connectivity and coherence.

d. Practice and rehearse

A good speaker is always prepared for his/her delivery and is confident of the content and the success of presentation. But when it comes to a new presenter under training period or a novice one, only practice and rehearsal can help him/her to develop his presentation skills. In order to become familiar with the content and flow of the topic, practice can help the presenter to improve his/her performance. One can do this in front of mirror or video record the practice session and keenly monitor whether the speaker is doing well or not. Such practice and rehearsal help a presenter to focus on his delivery, manage allotted time, maintain good body language and gestures, and take care of smooth delivery of presentation.

e. Body language and kinesics

'Action speaks louder than words' is a famous proverb in English. A good speaker pays proper attention to his body language and non-verbal communication which is also called as kinesics. The success of a presentation is not purely depended on the loaded content of the topic but how effectively the content is being presented by the speaker. A speaker should emphasise facial expressions, gestures, optical contacts, body movements, and kinesics in general.

f. Effective speaking and delivery

Effective presentation and delivery make a positive impression on the audience. A good speaker is very cautious of his/her speaking style. S/He clearly articulates the words, avoid rushing through the content, take pauses whenever needed, allow audience to ask questions and clarify doubts. A smooth delivery along with acceptable English grammar and communication can make the speaker successful.

g. Connect with the audience

The presenter's intellectual connect with the audience is necessary for the success of the presentation. The speaker should put in sincere efforts to establish a rapport with the audience by engaging them actively in the presentation. The speaker can encourage the audience through questions, interaction, activities, and so on. The speaker can incorporate short stories, anecdotes, examples, or some relevant content and relate the same with the audience.

h. Be confident and reliable

The vote of confidence and reliability are the assets of a presenter. The speaker should believe in his/her own capacity and knowledge so that his presentation becomes successful. Similarly, the presenter is expected to be trustworthy for his/her content that s/he shares with the audience. This self-confidence and trustworthiness make a presenter successful.

i. Time management

Time management is crucial for a presenter. Actually, human beings cannot manage time. On the contrary, we have to manage ourselves according to the available time. A speaker is allotted with a certain time span for his/her topic presentation. It is the responsibility of the speaker to manage according to the allotted time.

j. Learning from the feedback

After the presentation is over, ensure that you interact with the audience and clarify their doubts about the topic delivered. In addition, take feedback from the audience about your talk in the view to collect it for your self-improvement. Feedback is a tool that facilitates an individual for further growth and provides an opportunity to learn and relearn.

These are some of the tips to improve presentation skills. This type of skill is required for every professional today. In all sectors, presentation is inevitable and an individual should have necessary skill set in order to hone it and take it to the next level.

As a whole, presentation skills can be developed at any stage but your intensity to learn, practice and present are the necessary steps for success. A presenter who can understand the pulse of the audience can never fail on the floor.

15. Management Skills

A manager is not a person who can do the work better than his men; he is a person who can get his men to do the work better than he can.

-   Frederick W. Smith

Management skills are essential for every professional having a position with authority and responsibility in the hierarchy within an organization. Effective managerial skills involve human resource management, guiding and motivating teams, making strategic decisions, and achieving organizational goals. A manager is expected to be a person with dynamic personality who can handle diverse ups and downs by showing his decision-making ability in the nick of time.

Management skills have different categories which are based on various factors. A few common types of management are discussed below:

1. Functional Management

Functional management is a diverse domain of managerial responsibility. Organizations are divided into various functional areas depending on the specific work or domains such as human resource, finance, marketing, operations, crisis, strategic managements, etc. Generally, each functional area or work domain is managed by a specialized manager who looks into the activities and operations limited within the area or work domain.

2. Human Resource Management

A manager is a dynamic person who has the ability to identify competence in the workforce in an organization. Every individual is unique and has some or the other quality which has to be utilized for the benefit of the organization. A manager with better skills of identifying talent in the workforce can channelize human resource to reap benefits for organizational growth. The basic principle of human resource management is – the growth of an employee is equal to the growth of the organization. Based on this principle every individual employee is equally important irrespective of his or her work profile in the hierarchy.

3. Strategic Management

Strategic management is a level of management which has decision making power and formulate strategy for an organization in order to achieve its long-term goals. It includes strategic planning, resource allocation, and decision making at organizational level.

4. Operations Management

The organizations involved in production, supply chain, and overall operations focus on this type of managerial skill development. This type of management involves optimization of man power and resource generation, improving productivity, quality maintenance, and logistics management. The satisfaction of the customer in terms of quality product and in time delivery is the major focus areas of this type of management.

5. Project Management

Planning, organizing, controlling the resources and activities of an organization are the major focal areas of this type of management. The project managers look into the project initiation and completion. From project initiation to project completion goes through many phases and every stage or phase has equal importance.

6. Change Management

Every organization faces several changes and transformations time and again. Change management deals with managing organizational changes effectively. This type of management involves planning and implementation strategies to help individuals and teams to go through transitions smoothly. Change management plays a crucial role in restructuring, new technology implementation, mergers, new set-ups and so on.

7. Risk Management

Potential uncertainties and risks are the inevitable aspects of any organization. Risk management involves identifying, assessing, addressing, and mitigating potential risks in business. Addressing these risks related to financial, legal, operational, or environmental issues have to be tackled systematically and methodically. When you look at it logically, you will find that the difference between falling and flying is the risk management. Managing risk is more important than simply taking risk. Actually, it is not enough just to take risk but to optimize risk by weighing pros and cons and by reducing the probability of unexpected occurrence. Strong process of risk management can help to achieve your goals steadily and sustainably.

8. Quality Management

Quality assurance and quality maintenance are the top priorities of all business establishments. The organizations ensuring quality in products, services, processes, and put in their efforts to the expectations of the customers and consumers have vertical growth. The professional organizations appoint Quality Control Managers who look after implementing quality control measures, continuous improvement initiatives, adherence to quality standards and certificates.

9. Finance Management

Finance is the backbone of any business. Without financial support nothing can happen and move forward. Finance managers look into the organization's financial resources, budgeting, planning, income sources, investments, and reporting to the higher authorities. The performance of any organization is measured based on the financial condition and sustainability.

10. Team Management

Team performs with a basic principle of 'together everyone achieves more'. So, team management involves coordination among the members of a group or team putting efforts to achieve common goals. Team management includes team building, motivation, goal setting, strategy making, delegation, conflict resolution, communication and collaboration among the members of a team.

11. Crisis Management

Crisis, unexpected events, untoward happenings, and emergencies which may disrupt the routine normal operations of any organization need a team of managers who handle organizational crisis and any threat to the reputation and survival of the organization. The team of crisis managers involve in making contingency plans, communication strategies, quick decision making, and handle crisis situations systematically.

These are a few examples of the types of management. Many organizations combine different kinds of needs and shoulder the responsibility on the group of managers who handle these situations. There are a few organizations which customize management approaches based on their specific needs and industry and get the task done by the specified managers having exclusive professional skills.

The making of a successful manager is not theoretically possible in a business school but it is possible only in the real time experience of professional life. In the following sections, a few key management skills have been discussed. Inculcating these skills may be helpful to every budding manager:

a. Vision and strategic thinking

A manager should have a clear vision to his contribution to the growth of an organization. In addition, s/he should have short-term goals and a long-term vision for the organization. In order to achieve to the short-term goals and long-term vision, the manager should be very strategic and committed. Such managers understand a larger picture of the organization and can communicate a vision to a team by inspiring and motivating every member of a team to achieve the goals.

b. Communication skills

Communication skills in English are the success mantra today. Every individual living in personal or professional life needs effective communication skills in order to express in written or spoken context in different situations. In this professional and global world, communication skills in English have been considered very much important. Every manager managing several aspects of an organization has to communicate with different people from diverse background and countries hence English has occupied a prime position as a medium of communication all over the world. So, strong communication skills are crucial for managers in order to articulate their ideas clearly, listen actively, provide feedback, and foster open and effective communication within the team and outside the team.

c. Emotional intelligence

The managers with high emotional intelligence can develop strong relationship among the members of a team, execute their plan cordially, resolve conflicts and motivate team members effectively. Emotional intelligence incorporates self-awareness, empathy, and ability to understand one's emotions. All these aspects provide an opportunity to a manager to handle his team emotionally and professionally both.

d. Decision making

Decision making skill is also one of the most important requirements of a manager. The managers should be able analyse information, consider diverse perspectives, and assess pros and cons in order to make effective decisions. The managers also take up responsibility of their decisions and learn from the mistakes.

e. Delegation and empowerment

Effective managers represent their organization at different levels. They shoulder organizational responsibility and prove their strength and capabilities. Their ability of delegation becomes an asset of the team and the managers pass on their skills to other members. They put in their efforts to empower their team members by providing autonomy, resources, and support.

f. Conflict resolution

Conflicts are inevitable in all organizations. The managers those who have the ability to handle conflicts and resolve issues within the team contribute immensely to the organization. The skilled mangers have diverse skill set to tackle with the situations, discuss matters and find root cause of the problems, find an acceptable solution to the problems and get it done by collaboration and effective communication.

g. Motivation and inspiration

Managers motivate and inspire their team members to achieve their best performance. The managers are expected to identify every individual and their abilities. Motivation and encouragement by the people in the hierarchy make a big difference in the approach and attitude of the employees. The team member comes forward to perform their level best and put in their sincere efforts to achieve common goals.

h. Adaptability and resilience

Managers are expected to be flexible and adaptable in all circumstances. Uncertainty and unexpected changes are usually seen in all the organizations. The managers who are open to learn new things do accept changes in professional life. Such managers inspire resilience in their team especially during the period of adversity.

i. Team building and collaboration

Managers lead their team and have commanding positions. Their team building approach decides the success of the team and their efforts to achieve professional goals. Being a team leader, one should win the confidence of all the members and that will support the manager to take the team efforts to the next level. Building vote of trust for one another, encouraging diverse perspectives, respecting multi-cultural belonging, creating team values and ethics are some of the moves of a good and successful manager for collaborative work. They should have a quest for achieving common goals of the team and always build up a team spirit for each and every task assigned.

j. Continuous learning and improvement

Continuous learning is the sign of liveliness of an employee. This liveliness proves to be an asset to the organization. Effective and committed managers are passionate for their professional goals and growth. They take every opportunity as a challenge, learn new things in the course of dealing and continuously work for the organizational growth. So, continuous learning and improvement in each employee is always good for the organization.

Finally, one can say that developing managerial skills is an ongoing process. Real time experience teaches more than bookish knowledge. Effective managers can cultivate a strong work culture and drive an organization to success.

16. Universal Human Values

Appreciate those who love you. Help those who need you. Forgive those who hurt you. Forget those who leave you.

-   Gautam Buddha

Universal human values are the ethical principles and beliefs which are fundamental and shared by people belonging to different cultures, societies and religions. These values are treated as moral and ethical frameworks for human behaviour, guide people towards justified action, and promote common good of common all. There are specific values which are common across religions and cultures so they are called universal human values and commonly followed and appreciated throughout the world. Some of the universal human values are as follows:

1. Respect for Human Dignity

The nature has blessed human being with a developed brain and with this brain power; human beings have created so many things in the world. Across all the cultures, the principle of respecting human dignity is common. It entails treating others with courtesy, empathy, fairness, regardless of their background, cultures, religions, colour, gender, and social status.

2. Love and Compassion

According to some sociologists, love and compassion are interconnected and they are the fundamental values which are almost equally treated across all the cultures. Love is a deep affection of care for others which sometimes extend beyond the self. It involves a genuine concern for happiness, co-existence, fulfilment, and it can manifest in different ways for friends, family members, romantic partners, etc. Love also encourages the feeling of sacrifice and selflessness. Similarly, compassion is closely linked to the ability of an individual who empathize with the suffering and difficulties of others and get self-motivated to help and support others to come out of it. Compassion goes beyond pity and sympathy. It encourages action and stand in support for others. The feeling of compassion cultivates a sense of interconnectedness and foster concern and care. Love and compassion play a crucial role for harmonious survival that persuades betterment of all.

3. Empathy

Empathy involves understanding feelings, emotions, sentiments, difficulties and sufferings of other people. It also involves the desire for easing others sufferings and difficulties by promoting kindness and initiating a few efforts in this direction.

4. Honesty and Integrity

Honesty is the best policy. It involves being truthful, sincere, trustworthy in our actions, deeds, and words. Honesty is the foundation of building vote of trust and maintains the same for healthy relationship with others. Integrity means acting in accordance with one's values and ethics and stick up to the same in life even when nobody notices it.

5. Justice and Fairness

The principle of justice involves the idea of equality, impartiality, and the rule of natural law and law of the democratic state. According to the rule of natural law and law of the democratic state, it is ensured that everyone has equal opportunity to flourish and be treated justly. In addition, it also emphasises the need of fairness while dealing with different people.

6. Freedom and Autonomy

In all democratic countries, freedom and speech, thought, expression, religion, are treated as fundamental principles and every state ensures their citizen's freedom and autonomy. Freedom indicates an individual's ability of making a choice without any interference.

7. Tolerance

The principle of tolerance involves open-mindedness, dialogues, peaceful co-existence in diverse communities and cultures for the betterment of humanity. This principle also teachers us to accept opinion, beliefs, cultures, and lifestyle and reject the same for no reason peacefully.

8. Truth

The concept of truth is a quality of being or taking a stand based on the facts, evidence, or reality. It is a fundamental principle admired all over the world and encourages people to be trustworthy, fair and truthful all the time. Honesty, trustworthiness and being truthful are the interconnected qualities of an individual. The path of truthfulness is considered to be a tough one and it demands judgements and decisions based on facts, and evidences.

9. Non-violence and Peace

The principle of non-violence and non-aggression promotes the resolution of any conflict, promotion of justice, pursuit of social change without any harm and violence to any at all conditions. This philosophy encourages the principles of peace, empathy for others, and common good of common all. In our culture, we have Mahatma Gautam Buddha, Mahatma Mahavira, and Mahatma Gandhi as the apostles of peace and non-violence. This principle encompasses non-violent resistance, peaceful conflict resolution, advocates peace, righteousness and justice.

Peace is state of tranquillity, harmony, and absence of any conflict. This principle involves peaceful conditions within a country among the communities, between and among the countries and all over the world. It is a fundamental human aspiration and a means of conflict resolution. The opposite of peace is war and conflict. War is called as 'Worst Act of Reason'. War and conflict can never be a means of maintaining peace. Peace refers to a state of calmness, contentment, harmony, and cultivates positive mindfulness.

10. Service

The people who have love, compassion and empathy for others may develop a feeling of being supporting and helping others selflessly. Service involves the act of being kind, supportive to other and their well-being. This kind act brings difference in the lives of individuals, communities, or society. This principle can take various forms like volunteering, philanthropy and community works in the field of education, healthcare, and social works of different kind. Service has several key aspects like altruism, renunciation, social responsibility, sacrifice, compassion, empathy, love, spiritual enlightenment, etc.

11. Environmental Stewardship

Being the part and parcel of this Mother Nature, all the human beings have a commitment towards the nature that we have to protect the entire natural phenomenon. We should feel this interconnectedness of humanity and natural world around. We have to initiate sustainable scientific and technological development and protect environment and ensure the well-being of the future generations.

These are a few examples of universal human values related to our cultures, religions, and personal values also. All these values provide us a common background for moral, ethical and principled behaviour and encourage human beings to transcend our life by creating a difference and generate a new heritage for the upcoming generations.

Bibliography

Alex, K. *Soft Skills: Know Yourself and Know the World.* New Delhi: S. Chand and Company Limited, 2009.

Alex, K. Managerial Skills, S. Chand Publishing, ebook.https://www.google.co.in/books/edition/Managerial_Skills/ujJ lDwAAQBAJ?hl=en&gbpv=0

Brownell, J. *Listening: Attitudes, Principles and Skills.* Boston MA: Allyn and Bacon, 1996.

Burnard, Philip. *Interpersonal Skills Training.* New Delhi: Viva, 1995.

Butterworth, John & Thwaites, Geoff *Critical Thinking and Problem Solving*, Cambridge University Press, 2013.

Christopher, Elizabeth and Smith. *Leadership Training: A Sourcebook of Activities.* New Delhi: Viva, 1996.

Clark, Robert P. Global Awareness Thinking Systematically about the World, Rowman & Littlefield Publishers, 2002.

Dignen, Bob; Flinders, Steve and Sweeney, Simon. *For Work and Life English 365.*Cambridge University Press, Cambridge,2005.

Dinesh Babu, S. *Professional Ethics and Human Values*, Laxmi Publications Pvt. Ltd. 2007.

Goleman, Daniel. *Working with Emotional Intelligence*, Bloomsbury Publishing, 2009.

Hasson, Gill. Emotional Intelligence, Willey, 2019.

Julie Frechette, Rob Williams.*Media Education for a Digital Generation*, Taylor & Francis2015.

Lamb. "Non-verbal Communication." *www.essaymania.com* *Non-Verbal Communication*.

Kallet, Michael. *Think Smarter Critical Thinking to Improve Problem-Solving and Decision-Making Skills*, Wiley, 2014.

Mohan, Krishna and Raman, Meenakshi. *Effective English Communication.* New Delhi: Tata Mc-Graw Publishing Company Limited, 2000.

Mulidhar Koteshwar, PPT on *Leadership Skills, HRDC Goa.*

Mizrachi, Diane. et al. *Information Literacy: Lifelong Learning and Digital Citizenship in the 21st Century*, Second European Conference, ECIL 2014, Dubrovnik, Croatia, October 20-23, 2014. Proceedings, Springer International Publishing.

Narayanaswami, V.R. *Strengthen Your Writing.* Orient Longman, Chennai,1979.

"Non-Verbal Communication Modes" *andrews.edu.* BASD 560. Intercultural Business Relations 2011.

Noddings, Nel.Educating Citizens for Global Awareness, Teachers College Press,2005.

Pless, Nicola M. & Maak, Thomas. *Responsible Leadership.* Springer Netherlands, Germany. 2012.

Porter, G.W. "Non-verbal Communication." *www.essaymania.com* *Non-Verbal Communication*, n.d.

Raghvan, *Human Values and Professional Ethics: Text and Cases,* Wisdom Publications, 2012.

Rao, Ramakrishna A. *Learning English – A Communicative Approach.* Orient Longman Private Limited, Hyderabad,2005.

Richardson, Tim. *The Responsible Leader*, Kogan Page, 2015.

Ritts, Vicki. "Six Ways to Improve Your Non-verbal Communications." *www.honolulu.hawaii.edu* St. Louis Community College, Florissant Valley.

Rizvi, Ashraf M. *Effective Technical Communication.* New Delhi: Tata McGraw Hill, 2006.

Shah, Ken and Shah, Param J. "Making Effective Decisions." *www.laynetworks.com* Lay Networks.

Tom Elfring Ed. *Corporate Entrepreneurship and Venturing*, Springer US, 2005.

Tortoriello, Blott, and DeWine. *"Communicating Critical Thinking* Chapter 1: Communicating with others." *LAVC Jobs Program. www.laccriticalthinking.wordpress.com*

Yadava, Raju B. et al. *Building Competency: A Course in Reading and Writing English.* Guntur: Maruthi Publications, 2008.

Cover Design Courtesy: www.pixabay.com